IMAGES
of America

NEW LONDON
POLICE DEPARTMENT

Sr. Sgt. Lawrence M. Keating is pictured as a rookie sitting inside his patrol car with the interior light on him, alone with his thoughts as he completes paperwork yet always in the public spotlight. His field training officer, Lonnie de la Cruz, took this photograph. Keating has made patrols on foot, bicycle, motorcycle, and boat in the six-square-mile city with the Thames River as a border. New London maintains an intricate history of famous and wealthy leaders from land and sea, as well as ruffians and transients, immigrants, sailors and soldiers, Coast Guard cadets, and college students. There have been abolitionists and bigots among the brown, black, white, and intermarried homeowners, tenants, teachers, addicts, business owners, and preachers—and ensured fair rights for many. The city has called upon its police force to help drowning victims from docks, beaches, and sinking boats and bridge jumpers; safeguard crowds at fireworks and festivals, during parades, and on routes of children going to school and their after-school sporting events; and respond to shootings and stabbings, drug and rum runners, prostitutes, the insane, the abandoned and neglected infants and children. The police have also been first responders to fires, accidents, false alarms, traffic jams, fender benders, and lost pets. They have contended with agendas that were meant to fit the means and ends of property owners near and far. They have done so under all weather conditions and while trying to raise families of their own, be good spouses and neighbors, and manage the immense stress this job brings with it. The city's tough and complicated history has been kept in check by the New London police officers who are woven in every fiber of every event in the Whaling City. (Author's collection.)

ON THE COVER: The New London Police color guard, pictured in the 1950s, marches in the lead of one of the many parades in New London. The officers, from left to right, are Joseph Gaffney, Herb Moran, Roger DuPont (carrying weapon), Jack Heard, Louis Pine (presenting US flag), unidentified, Sgt. William Riordin (leading), John Miceli (flag bearer), John Crowley, Daniel Murphy (carrying rifle), and Henry J. McIninch. (Courtesy of the Riordan-Manavas-Lewis families.)

IMAGES
of America

NEW LONDON
POLICE DEPARTMENT

Sr. Sgt. Lawrence M. Keating,
Lawrence Keating, and Catherine Keating

ARCADIA
PUBLISHING

Published by Arcadia Publishing
Charleston, South Carolina

Printed in the United States of America

Library of Congress Control Number: 2019937601

For all general information, please contact Arcadia Publishing:
Telephone 843-853-2070
Fax 843-853-0044
E-mail sales@arcadiapublishing.com
For customer service and orders:
Toll-Free 1-888-313-2665

Visit us on the Internet at www.arcadiapublishing.com

*To the New London police officers who uphold their
duty to protect and serve: Thank you. We are proud of
you. May God bless you and God bless America!*

CONTENTS

ACKNOWLEDGMENTS

We thank Chief of Police Peter G. Reichard; retirees Sgt. Harry Chiappone, Capt. Kenneth W. Edwards Jr., Lt. William Lacey Jr., and Master Patrol Officer (MPO) Les Smith Jr.; former officer Phillip Fazzino and the New London County State's Attorney's Office; and MPO Roger Baker. Unless otherwise noted, all images appear courtesy of the authors. We thank Arcadia Publishing, Susan Cavanaugh Chmielewski, Michael Cavanaugh, Donald Chieco, Luanne Wells DeMatto, Louise Mugovero Dickens, Timothy and Paul Foley, Ann Marie Keating, Margaret Mary Riordin Manavas, Joan Corcoran McIntire, Neil and Elaine Jullarine Moriarty, Thomas Moriarty, the Paskewich family, Georgette Pearson and Diane Pearson Rossi, Annemarie Sheehan, Marcia Stuart (researcher and retired librarian), Dr. John Sullivan, Clark van der Lyke (retired New London city clerk), Renée Vogt, George Wong, New London Police Union Local 724, New London City clerk/registrar of vital statistics Jonathan Ayala and staff, Darrin Villafana of A. Secondino & Son, Inc., Jay's Photoshop in Old Saybrook, ABC Photos in Mystic, and the staff at A.C. Moore and Staples on Frontage Roads in New London.

We thank officers who served in our military on active duty full-time and for the state part-time. We acknowledge that most had served in some capacity for the service until the draft ended in 1973. We have tried to acknowledge all those after that time period as we were informed.

Information in parts of this book was verified from *New London Goes to War: New London during World War II, 1941–1945* by Clark van der Lyke through the New London County Historical Society; the *Bee*, the *Day*, and the *Norwich Bulletin*; *The Day Paper: The Story of One of America's Last Independent Newspapers* by Gregory Stone; *Passbook to a Proud Past and a Promising Future* by the Society for Savings; US Library of Congress; *A Diverse People: Connecticut, 1914 to the Present* by Herbert F. Janick Jr.; *Preachers, Rebels, and Traders: Connecticut, 1818 to 1865* by Janice Law Trecker through the Pequot Press Publications; *County Government in Connecticut: Its History and Demise* by Rosaline Levenson for the Institute of Public Service; *The Old Whaling Port* by Charlotte Molyneux Holloway; *History of New London* by Frances Manwaring Caulkins; *African American Connecticut Explored*, published by Wesleyan University Press; *Connecticut Explored*; *Celebrate Connecticut 350 Years*, edited by David M. Roth and Judith Arnold Grenier in 1986, by the Connecticut Historical Commission; Postcard History Series: *New London* and Images of America: *Connecticut State Police*; *The People of Connecticut* by Warren J. Halliburton; *History of Eastern Connecticut* by Pliny LeRoy Harwood; *New London Police History* by Richard B. Wall, which was issued for the Gymnasium and Library Fund in 1917; and the *New London Directories*.

INTRODUCTION

In 2018, the officers of the New London, Connecticut, Police Department celebrated 150 years of consistent policing in the Whaling City. Its officers reflect the cultural diversity of its citizens, and many were and continue to be the Irish. Due to the high activity of ships in and out of the port, the military bases and academies of the Navy, Coast Guard and US Merchant Marines, the former Army posts of Fort Terry and Fort Trumbull, and the railroad workers and riders, female, Jewish, Italian, Polish, African American, West Indians, Latino, Hawaiian, Greek, and Filipino people have been employed. There were sheriffs and constables, supernumeraries, and permanent officers who served New London town and city. It would be nearly impossible to identify firsts, so it has not been broached in this publication.

In 1645, New London (so named in 1658) was settled along the Thames River. It was incorporated as a city in 1784. Constables were carryovers from England and hired on an as-needed basis. A sheriff system was established until officers were needed in the mid-1800s. The department continues to be on the books in city hall as a police force. Richard B. Wall writes that there had been constables and sheriffs for the city and the town, with one of the earliest dates of appointments of sheriffs being in the mid-1660s.

In 1853 and 1860, failed attempts were made to establish a night watch. The Civil War came and went, except for the soldiers and deserters who often caused trouble in the city. Constables were hired for 20 days at a time and were called up as needed, not having a regular route to patrol. Starting in 1863, councilman Dr. Henry Potter was in charge of and referred to as the chief of the police department for $1 per day. Each month, he was to report to the court of common council (today's city council). In 1863, there were two police officers—Frederick Freese and Clinton Shepard—with another officer added a year later. The Pequot House and summer resort area were attracting many visitors each summer, with the politically powerful and wealthy making up the Pequot Colony. By November 1864, the number of police officers had decreased, and the request for a permanent police building was transferred for review to the public property committee. Criminals were brought to the almshouse or held in private homes. Eventually, the prisoners were held in cells in a brick building near the Neptune block or in the city hall building.

In 1864, the council voted to establish a permanent police force with Dr. Potter as superintendent. They were called the police, were issued scant gear, met for assignments in city hall, and used the selectmen's room for police court. By June 1865, the year the Civil War ended and slavery was abolished, there was a vote not to have a permanent police force due to ill will relating to politics between the mayor and the council over allegiance to the presidential candidates. In December 1865, the council voted not to fund a police force and to return to a constable system, with a sheriff in town. Prominent citizen T.W. Williams protested, and it was delayed six months until June 1866.

Finally, the townspeople voted to fund the police with a permanent night watch, funded with $700 and additional money authorized to purchase a 25-by-65-foot lot on the east side of Potter

Street. A police station was built with a lower floor of eight cells, an office, a squad room, and the tramp room on the second floor. This would remain the police department for almost 30 years, until 1897. By 1905, there were no longer any sheriffs listed in the directories for the city of New London.

In 1868, a permanent police force began with a night watch of George P. Hinckley (sometimes spelled Hinkley), Andrew "A.J." Quinn, John L. Ward, George R. Kimberly, and J.C. Shepard. They logged in 191 arrests for "offences" [sic] such as "adultery, breach of beach, theft, and disturbing religious meetings." In 1869, the new station house cost $4,809.35 and was placed into the care of Sheriff R. Addams. The police reported 266 arrests for offenses such as "breach of peace, attempting to break into cabin of sloop, attempting to poison, and breaking door in night season." The earliest day-shift officers were Hezekiah B. Smith and John White. White (whose grandson was Sgt. John E. White, page 70) served for 30 years under Captains Hinckley, Quinn, and George Haven. White was lieutenant for 20 years except for several months as captain in 1894. In 1875, the annual report complimented the overworked officers, who made 651 arrests that year. Added to the rolls in the upcoming years were Joseph A. Burrows and Charles F. Freese. By 1877, H.S. Bartlett was appointed health officer. Some officers doubled as detectives, but one early detective was Charles P. Hammond. In 1899, the average arrest per officer was 144. New Haven officers averaged 72 and Norwich 64.

The chiefs were called captains until 1946. Funding has intermittently been provided for motorcycles, K-9s, boats, and bicycles. There has always been an animal control division. To become a permanent officer, a candidate had to clear a physical and go through training to get on a list as a supernumerary. The last round of supernumeraries was in the 1980s.

In 2018, the police headquarters sits at 5 Governor Winthrop Boulevard on the corner of Eugene O'Neill Drive (formerly known as Main Street). It is a secure building with a sally port. Fire and police dispatchers are able to send loudspeaker notifications to the public and "ping" the location of cell phones. Officers patrol on foot, bicycle, motorcycle, with dogs, and in cars and sport utility vehicles (SUVs). They travel with portable and fixed radios, computers, and cameras to communicate with citizens in person or via social media.

One

1800s–1930s

Police officers march west up State Street around 1930 with a motorcycle officer in the lead. An ordinance in 1915 allowed police authority to limit vehicles driving through parades. In 1933, there were 48 patrolmen and a patrolwoman. During this decade, officers received new uniforms. The first permanent license plates were issued in the state, and women sat on a jury for the first time. (Courtesy of the New London Police Union.)

Capt. George P. Hinckley led the force from 1872 to 1878, resigned, went to sea, and returned in 1883. He was paid per trip to transport boys or men to the reform school or insane asylum in addition to his small annual salary. He requested "iron to replace shredded boards between cells" in the jail. Sealing ships to Kerguelen were operating out of New London and sending oil back to the city. (Courtesy of the New London Police Department.)

Andrew J. "A.J." Quinn was captain from 1879 to 1883. Wages decreased his first year to $70 per month, and patrolmen's wages decreased to $60, but they were offered a week's paid vacation. To save money, officers lit and extinguished gas streetlamps. By 1879, there were 2,014 inoperable gas or naphtha lamps. Quinn, a beloved leader, had a full police escort to the cemetery when he died in January 1884. (Courtesy of the Public Library of New London.)

State Street is seen in this c. 1850s–1870s view looking east towards the Thames River at Main Street. On March 11, 1880, an obituary was in the *Morning Journal and Courier* for native and city physician Dr. Henry Potter, born in 1825; he graduated from Yale Medical School in 1866, and during part of the Civil War, he was captain of the police of New London. In 1903, there was a request for five patrolmen, a patrol wagon, and a signal system. Capt. George Haven reported that officers had to carry helpless men long distances to keep them from freezing to death, and there was a daily parade of unsavory and scantily clothed men and women because the police had to rely upon express wagons, hacks, or baggage trucks borrowed from the railroad station. By 1925, streets were widened, and uniform signs for parking were attached to arc streetlamps. In 1943, a movie was filmed in parts of New London entitled *Destination Tokyo*, with Cary Grant. (Photograph by Giles Bishop; courtesy of the Public Library of New London.)

11

Capt. George Haven, shown here in 1882, led from 1888 to 1918. In 1908, he earned just over $1,600 per month. The station house budget at North Bank Street was $1,200 for the year. The city directory lists him as a private serving in the Civil War with the US Army, 1st Battalion, Connecticut Cavalry, Company C. He would go on to retire as a brigadier general. In 1897, he was the adjutant general for the state. He served when there was a downward turn on Wall Street and voter fraud through bribery ushered in voting machines. Locally, he refers to a "thin line" of officers who maintained the area from Mohegan Avenue to the lighthouse. The day-shift officers spent several days a month distributing paychecks. In his annual report, he expressed his opinion that officers should not be used as "messenger boys." He requested more officers as well as a better means of communication with beat patrols to and from police headquarters. (Courtesy of the New London Police Department.)

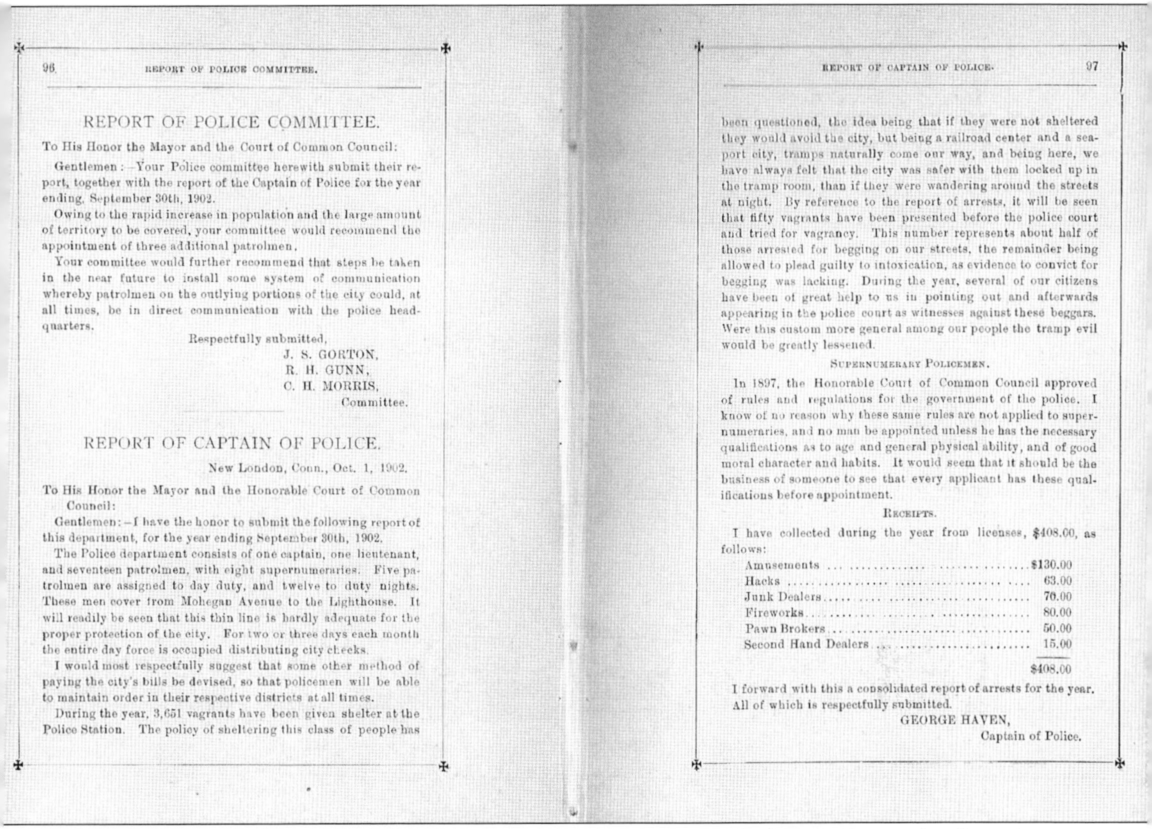

REPORT OF POLICE COMMITTEE.

To His Honor the Mayor and the Court of Common Council:

Gentlemen:—Your Police committee herewith submit their report, together with the report of the Captain of Police for the year ending, September 30th, 1902.

Owing to the rapid increase in population and the large amount of territory to be covered, your committee would recommend the appointment of three additional patrolmen.

Your committee would further recommend that steps be taken in the near future to install some system of communication whereby patrolmen on the outlying portions of the city could, at all times, be in direct communication with the police headquarters.

Respectfully submitted,
J. S. GORTON,
R. H. GUNN,
C. H. MORRIS,
Committee.

REPORT OF CAPTAIN OF POLICE.

New London, Conn., Oct. 1, 1902.

To His Honor the Mayor and the Honorable Court of Common Council:

Gentlemen:—I have the honor to submit the following report of this department, for the year ending September 30th, 1902.

The Police department consists of one captain, one lieutenant, and seventeen patrolmen, with eight supernumeraries. Five patrolmen are assigned to day duty, and twelve to duty nights. These men cover from Mohegan Avenue to the Lighthouse. It will readily be seen that this thin line is hardly adequate for the proper protection of the city. For two or three days each month the entire day force is occupied distributing city checks.

I would most respectfully suggest that some other method of paying the city's bills be devised, so that policemen will be able to maintain order in their respective districts at all times.

During the year, 3,651 vagrants have been given shelter at the Police Station. The policy of sheltering this class of people has

been questioned, the idea being that if they were not sheltered they would avoid the city, but being a railroad center and a seaport city, tramps naturally come our way, and being here, we have always felt that the city was safer with them locked up in the tramp room, than if they were wandering around the streets at night. By reference to the report of arrests, it will be seen that fifty vagrants have been presented before the police court and tried for vagrancy. This number represents about half of those arrested for begging on our streets, the remainder being allowed to plead guilty to intoxication, as evidence to convict for begging was lacking. During the year, several of our citizens have been of great help to us in pointing out and afterwards appearing in the police court as witnesses against these beggars. Were this custom more general among our people the tramp evil would be greatly lessened.

SUPERNUMERARY POLICEMEN.

In 1897, the Honorable Court of Common Council approved of rules and regulations for the government of the police. I know of no reason why these same rules are not applied to supernumeraries, and no man be appointed unless he has the necessary qualifications as to age and general physical ability, and of good moral character and habits. It would seem that it should be the business of someone to see that every applicant has these qualifications before appointment.

RECEIPTS.

I have collected during the year from licenses, $408.00, as follows:

Amusements	$130.00
Hacks	63.00
Junk Dealers	70.00
Fireworks	80.00
Pawn Brokers	50.00
Second Hand Dealers	15.00
	$408.00

I forward with this a consolidated report of arrests for the year. All of which is respectfully submitted.

GEORGE HAVEN,
Captain of Police.

In 1876, the commissioner of charities, William H. Starr, requested more money for the infirm who were very ill and " 'dropped' here from other towns." In 1890, Capt. George Haven reported the station being used as a "Lockup, Hospital, Morgue, and Dog pound" as well as a temporary holding place for the violently insane. He stated, "it offers very poor accommodations as a Hospital." The police department had just hooked up its cesspool vault to a sewer, but by 1897, it was called a "black hole" by the *Morning Telegraph*. In 1899, funding was approved for a new police station. In the interim, city hall was used for police headquarters. For several years, Haven requested "a combined patrol wagon and ambulance." In 1906, he wrote, "very often men badly injured lay for an hour or more waiting conveyance to the hospital," and in 1909, he wanted a "police patrol wagon quartered at police headquarters and used by police only because it is used as an ambulance because people think it belongs to the city and is free, but the stable charges for a driver and hitching up outside the use of police work and taken from the station house budget." Pictured above are two pages from the 1902 *Annual Report to the Common Council*.

Pictured in 1910 inside the squad room at the North Bank Street Station are, from left to right, (first row) Commissioner Ernest Cooney, Joseph F. Damas, Thomas Kiely, Commissioner John J. Ryan, Charles L. Waterman, Mayor Bryan Francis Mahan, Benjamin E. White, Commissioner Col. Eugene T. Kirkland, Timothy Sheehan (nights), Capt. George Haven, Sgt. Benjamin A. Beebe (nights), and Lt. Thomas J. Jeffers; (second row) Timothy T. Sullivan (nights), Timothy C. Sullivan (nights), James D. Gaffney (who would become a sergeant on nights in 1917), James C.

Sullivan (who ran the station house and would become a sergeant on day shift), Charles A. Pinney (who became a regular patrolman in 1909 and would go on to be captain of the force from 1918 to 1933; his station was located at 57 Bradley Street), Fred A. Manchester, Walter Rehn (nights), George Randall (holding station cat), Michael Corcoran (nights), Michael B. O'Neill (nights), Joseph Walter, David Nagle, and Cornelius D. Leary (keeper of the police station).

Michael J Corcoran

New London Connecticut Police Dept.

1896 - 1927

Patrolman Michael J. Corcoran was born in Ireland on May 10, 1865. He was a clerk before his appointment as a supernumerary in 1897. He was promoted to patrolman at the age of 35. He retired on May 1, 1927. The population of the city increased from 13,757 in 1890 to 17,548 in 1900 and to 29,640 in 1930. Corcoran started when the city had 30 wharves, 33 barbers, 10 blacksmiths, 6 bootblacks, a cracker manufacturer, 17 churches for 12 different denominations, 65 dressmakers, 107 grocers, 8 hat and cap makers, 3 businesses selling hay and straw, 2 hospitals, 11 hotels, 5 ice dealers, 13 jewelers, 17 laundries, 10 milk dealers, 2 pawnbrokers, 67 saloons (25 on Bank Street, 6 on State Street, and 5 on Main Street), 50 shoe dealers, 2 telegraph companies, the Southern New England Telephone Company (SNET), 4 theaters, and an umbrella repairer. Arrests for crimes that were unique to his era including the enforcement of the 1908 ordinance that "no pigs could be kept within the city limits without a permit" and the crimes of "cutting hawser, having beer bottles 'not his own,' buggery, spitting in a streetcar, selling oleomargarine illegally, violation of bylaws of Cedar Grove Cemetery, selling bob veal, and digging holes in Maple Avenue." (Courtesy of the New London Police Department.)

16

In this 1910 image, Sgt. Benjamin A. Beebe (center, facing building) talks with an unidentified patrolman. Beebe was a roundsman (who makes rounds in order to provide backup to officers on their beat) and, at times, a plains clothes officer. The man walking on the right is wearing a bowler hat. While it cannot be confirmed for this photograph, plains clothes officers often wore bowlers. In 1923, policewoman Alice Hunt served as a protective officer. She reported on 754 calls in her first six months. In April 1924, she was joined by Jane E. Cassidy, widow of Dr. Patrick Cassidy Jr. of Norwich. A probation officer position was established and filled by Richard W. Mansfield in 1925. (Courtesy of the Public Library of New London.)

STATE STREET—VIEW FROM THE UNION DEPOT.

This pre-1892 view of State Street looks west upon the Liberty Pole and flagpole. Poorly working kerosene streetlights were lit and extinguished by officers. Around 1895, tramps wandered the country and could get abusive when demanding assistance from citizens for handouts, so the police expanded to cover more areas at night. (Courtesy of the Public Library of New London.)

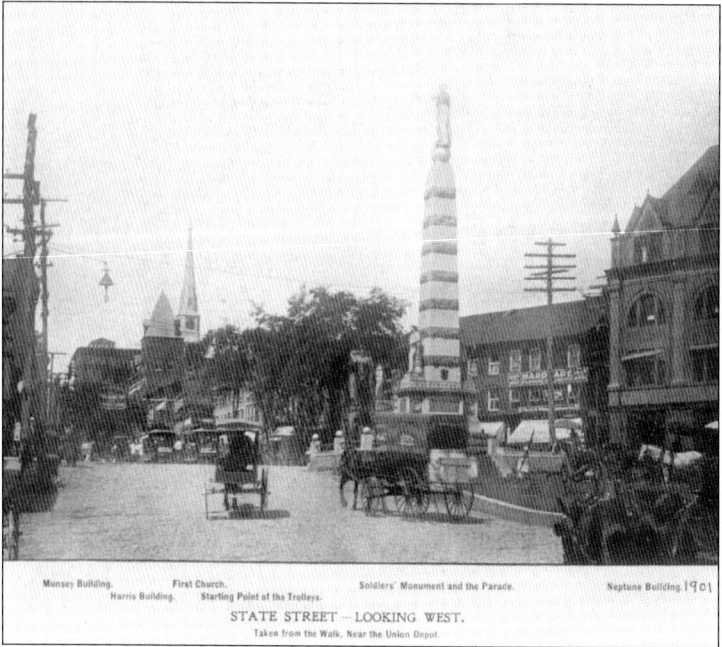

Munsey Building.　　First Church.　　　　Soldiers' Monument and the Parade.　　　Neptune Building. 1901
　　Harris Building.　　Starting Point of the Trolleys.
STATE STREET—LOOKING WEST.
Taken from the Walk, Near the Union Depot.

This c. 1901 image of State Street looks west at the Soldiers and Sailors Monument in the center of the parade. Officer H.S. Bartlett escorted the city physician to houses and businesses as an enforcer of health laws. In Bartlett's report to the city council, he requested an ordinance to force property owners to hook up to the city sewer system, because vaults in their yards contributed to ill health. (Courtesy of the Public Library of New London.)

Frank Lenehan, shown standing in 1912, would go on to become a sergeant with the force (see page 32). Walter Vogt is the young boy sitting in the wagon, and the horse is Nellie. Located at 78–80 Truman Street, the New England Bakery would become Vogt's Bakery. (Courtesy of George Wong.)

Franklin Street Jail is seen here in 1957. It was erected in 1845 with 16 cells (42 more cells were added in 1876). At first, it had no heat and was divided between the drunks and the 1,100–2,600 tramps housed annually. Prisoners came from the closed Norwich Hill Jail from 1953 until about 1960, when 55 prisoners were sent to the county jail in Montville. Shiloh Baptist Church took up services here in December 1963. (Photograph by Bishop & Kenyon; courtesy of the Public Library of New London.)

In this photograph, Officer Patrick Sheehan appears to be wearing badge No. 22. He retired wearing No. 1 after 34 years. His sons Eugene, John, and Dennis (see pages 68–69) followed in his footsteps. He started with the police department when Lawrence Hospital and St. Joseph's Church were built around 1910, the local Boy Scouts began, and the Connecticut Fraternal Order of Police was founded. (Courtesy of the John, Dennis, and Eugene Sheehan families.)

Thomas J. Jeffers is shown in 1918 wearing his lieutenant cap but was captain until December that year, when he retired after 30 years with a pension of $62.50 per month. In 1915, there were 100 licenses for hacks and jitneys but nothing to manage motorized vehicles. In 1917, World War I drew an influx of military personnel to the city, prompting a request for 10 more officers. (Courtesy of the New London Police Department.)

In the 1920s, Officer Wilbur Lewis (wearing No. 1 on his hat) is fourth from left at a roundhouse that was used for police and fire officers at Ocean Beach. A parklet known as Lewis Woods at the east end of the city was purchased by the city in 1893 and became Ocean Beach Park. This area was destroyed by the 1938 hurricane, and a new Ocean Beach was funded by the city in 1939. The park opened in 1940 and had an 87-foot clock tower. (Courtesy of the Public Library of New London.)

New London police officers are pictured with two trucks of seized bootleg liquor in the 1920s. In 1919, the 18th Amendment abolished the sale of liquor. Locally, the railroad bridge was converted into a vehicle bridge to Groton. Temperance groups formed, but efforts failed with gangs and speakeasies—aided by increased use of vehicles to transport bootleg liquor—and lack of interest in enforcing the law. In 1933, the 21st Amendment abolished the prohibition of liquor. (Courtesy of the New London Police Union.)

Officer Edward Henry Riordan, shown wearing Badge No. 23, was a World War I Army veteran who became a regular within seven months of joining the force in 1924. While on patrol at Ocean Beach, a gun pointed to his head misfired. In 1929, he responded to an armed robbery, was shot twice, returned fire, and continued chasing the perpetrator until collapsing. The robber was "found down" from his injuries the next day at Lake Konomoc with a bullet wound. For Riordan's efforts, he was awarded a medal for distinctive service. In 1942, he made sergeant. After multiple abdominal surgeries and due to hip pain from the shooting, he would become desk sergeant until his retirement after 30 years. Unfortunately, fragments from the two bullets created health issues and likely contributed to death at the age of 73. His brother William retired from the force, as did his son-in-law John Manavas, godson William D. Dittman Sr., and great-nephews Michael and William Lacey Jr. (Courtesy of the Public Library of New London.)

Sgt. Samuel Hick, wearing badge No. 12 around the 1920s, started as a city sheriff and became a regular patrolman on May 3, 1915. In January 1919, he replaced Lt. Thomas Jeffers, the same year World War I soldiers returned to New London from Europe, the National Prohibition Act (Volstead Act) went into effect, and women's right to vote passed (it was ratified in 1920). (Courtesy of the Public Library of New London.)

Frank J. Philopena wears badge No. 19 around the 1920s. In 1921, the city charter and manager took effect, replacing 18 aldermen with five wards. In November 1923, Capt. Charles A. Pinney reported that a new police Studebaker was used for service and charitable work. An ordinance curtailed the authority of the city manager over the police department, to which the city manager was opposed. (Courtesy of the Public Library of New London.)

The back of this photograph reads, "Al 'Whitey' Iverson, 'The Kiddin Kopper.' " He stands on a platform between trolley tracks on the corner of Main and State Streets. In the background is Union Station. This photograph was taken around the 1920s. His granddaughter would become Priscilla Presley. (Courtesy of the New London Police Department.)

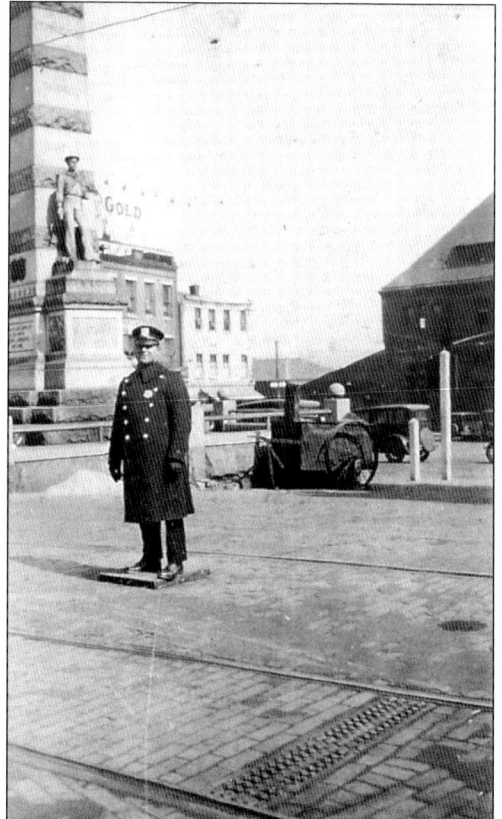

Carlos Stone is pictured near the Soldiers and Sailors Monument around 1929. He was also a motorcycle patrolman. He served during openings of synagogues located on Shapley Street and Blinman Street and near Ocean Beach. After restrictions on all religions allowed in city limits were lifted, the Jewish Society was legally allowed to form in New London (and the state of Connecticut) in 1843. A Jewish cemetery plot had been purchased in Cedar Grove Cemetery in 1878. (Courtesy of the New London Police Department.)

On October 15, 1927, officers march towards Mercer Field for a dedication ceremony. Mercer Field was nicknamed "Cannonball Park" and is located on the town line with Waterford. (Presented by the Bulkeley School Athletic Association; courtesy of the Public Library of New London.)

An unidentified officer appears to be keeping his balance during flooding when a storm hit near Ocean Beach in November 1932. In 1928, a police substation was organized at Ocean Beach and comprised 17 officers. (Courtesy of the Public Library of New London.)

In this image from the mid- to late 1930s, Capt. William T. Babcock can be seen on the far right (in the suit), and two state police officers assist Boy Scouts with bicycle inspections. The Boy Scouts were often involved in various police-related community events. In the mid- to late 1800s, the Colt Army Revolver, sewing machines, and bicycles were mass produced in Hartford, Connecticut. (Courtesy of the Public Library of New London.)

An unidentified child (left) wears a police cap as part of a uniform and appears to be directing traffic around 1930. The first Christmas toy sold in New London was in 1848 at the J.N. Harris store. (Courtesy of the Bruhns-Wells-Courtney family.)

Patrolman George Robert Bruhns, shown at the age of 27, wears badge no. 44 in this 1929 photograph. He was a regular in 1930. In 1956, he joined Det. Dennis J. Murphy and Lt. Thomas L. Cavanaugh as a detective. After 30 years, Bruhns requested retirement into the Veteran Reserve in 1958, because he had turned 55 years old and was required to retire per city ordinance. (Courtesy of the Bruhns-Wells-Courtney family.)

Braxton W. Hill stands outside city hall around 1929 wearing a traditional winter uniform of the times, including a nightstick that hangs on his left side. He became a private detective and played a major role in making life better for the city's children through the Knot Hole Gang (see page 52). In 1929, the Great Depression began. (Courtesy of the Public Library of New London.)

William J. Corcoran is seen here in the 1930s in a motorcycle uniform. He was a World War I Army veteran who fought in the Battles of Belleau Wood, Chateau Thierry, and Argonne. He was granted leave for four years to serve in the Coast Guard during World War II. He was a patrolman, motorcycle officer, plain clothes officer, and desk sergeant. By retirement, he had served 43 years with the force, and he turned 65 on his last day. (Courtesy of Joan Corcoran McIntire.)

Francis J. Corcoran, shown in uniform in 1930, worked four years as a supernumerary during the summers at Ocean Beach and then became the custodian at headquarters for 24 years. He had six known saves from attempted hangings by prisoners in their cells and was known for his kindness. Some ex-cons wrote to him after their release to express their gratitude. His son William J. Corcoran is pictured above, and his grandson worked in records for the force (see pages 29 and 81). (Courtesy of Joan Corcoran McIntire.)

William F. Corcoran is photographed in the 1940s, when he was a records clerk for the department. He left for several years but returned (see page 81). He was the third generation of his family to serve the city of New London. His father was retired Officer William J. Corcoran, and his grandfather was Francis J. Corcoran. (Courtesy of Joan Corcoran McIntire.)

Pictured around the 1930s is the police headquarters (from 1898 to 1948) on North Bank Street/Bradley Street with an unidentified officer. One officer who would have worked at this headquarters was James Daniel Gaffney (see page 14), who started, at age 30 in 1900, as a supernumerary for six years before being hired as a regular for 38 years; he retired as a lieutenant. When he was a young patrolman, he single-handedly broke up fights rather than arrest the fighters. He boxed Norwich officer Barney Keenan for 20 rounds to a draw. The two were friends in the years that followed the match. (Courtesy of the New London Police Union.)

This 1890 photograph shows State Street facing east. The library would be erected on the near right. The trolley ties shown in the gutter on the lower left of the photograph would be used to support tracks. *The New England Almanac and Farmer's Friend 1860*, published and sold by C. Prince at 4 Main Street in this city, reported "Set Shade Trees. . . . There are many things that it will do to delay. . . . No so, however, in setting out shade trees." In 1924, the trees were removed. (Courtesy of the Public Library of New London.)

On September 6, 1931, an officer facing east from the top of State Street maintains order with pedestrian, vehicle, and trolley traffic during the sesquicentennial celebration of the city. In 1924, "beacons of the mushroom type" were posted in Courthouse Square (left of the officer). The patrolman's orders supersede any lighted augmentation. The road is paved in Hillside brick, replacing the Belgian block placed in 1880. The library would be on the right. On the near left is the Garde Theater, with *The Common Law* advertised on the marquee. (Courtesy of the Public Library of New London.)

30

This squad picture was taken around 1930. In 1931, the police department was on 57 North Bank Street with one captain, one lieutenant, six sergeants, 38 patrolmen, and three supernumeraries. In 1936, the patrolmen had two days a month off and poor pay. It took until 1951 to have a five-day week. Advocating for better working conditions were officers William Corcoran, Walter Rehn, Clarence Martin, and Cornelius Moriarty. (Courtesy of the Riordan-Manavas-Lewis families.)

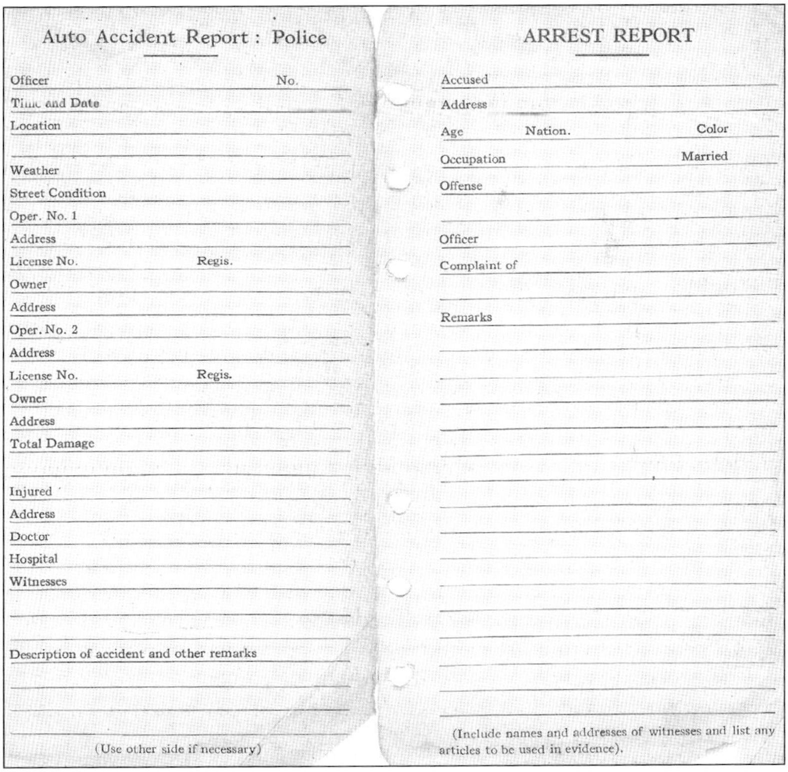

These pages are from a 1933 loose-leaf book. Report sheets could be hand-written on at the scene and removed or typed on at the station. The officer would write an investigative report on a lined sheet in this notebook (not shown) and then fill out details on the auto accident or arrest report sheets (shown at right). (Courtesy of Sr. Sgt. Kevin McBride and the Paskewich family.)

Auto Accident Report : Police

Officer	No.
Time and Date	
Location	
Weather	
Street Condition	
Oper. No. 1	
Address	
License No.	Regis.
Owner	
Address	
Oper. No. 2	
Address	
License No.	Regis.
Owner	
Address	
Total Damage	
Injured	
Address	
Doctor	
Hospital	
Witnesses	

Description of accident and other remarks

(Use other side if necessary)

ARREST REPORT

Accused	
Address	
Age	Nation.	Color
Occupation	Married
Offense	
Officer	
Complaint of	
Remarks	

(Include names and addresses of witnesses and list any articles to be used in evidence).

31

Officer Frank Lenehan is pictured here on Bank Street after the hurricane of 1938, when many local families lost loved ones and cottages near Ocean Beach were annihilated. In 1939, there were 4,504 arrests reported, with 2,556 traffic violations and one murder. Due to an influx of workers for World War II, there was inadequate and overcrowded housing, especially for minorities. Trolley tracks were pulled up and used towards the war effort. (Courtesy of David Morrison.)

Officer Dennis W. Cavanaugh is seen in front of 31 Vauxhall Street, Beechwood Manor, in the early 1950s. He began his career in 1917 with his brother Thomas, joining eldest brother John. One of Dennis's first assignments was Ocean Beach, and he would take a trolley to and from his patrol detail. In 1928, buses began to replace trolley travel, which ended in 1936 in New London. (Courtesy of Joel F. Riley.)

Two

1940s

From left to right are (first column) Army soldier Daniel Murphy, unidentified, Dennis Sheehan, Joseph Jullarine, Walter O'Neil, two unidentified, Charles Davidson, Ray Griswold, and Frank J. Philopena; (second column) Arthur Feeley, John Miceli, Kenny Ellwood, unidentified, K.T. Bucko, Neil Donahue, Harold Street, Salvatore Trafaconda, unidentified, and Paul Moriski. Murphy, with 10th Armored Division under General Patton, assisted with liberating concentration camps. Originating from multi-cultural Hodges Square/East New London, Murphy comforted detainees in their native tongue of Polish. (Courtesy of Neil and Elaine Jullarine Moriarty.)

Det. Sgt. John J. "Jack" Cavanaugh is seen around 1941. As a standout athlete, he was recruited by Capt. George Haven, who gave him a hat, flashlight, gun, and handcuffs and sent him on his beat as a supernumerary in 1915. He was one of the first motorcycle officers and retired as a lieutenant. A career highlight included climbing through a window of a moving train to chase a criminal atop 14 cars until reaching the Niantic Bridge, when Cavanaugh pulled his gun and ordered the man to jump into the bay, where the criminal was apprehended. In 1979, a television show recreated that chase in *Disaster on the Coastliner*. John's relatives on the force include brothers Thomas and Dennis, sons Eugene and Ronald, and grandsons Russell and Michael. During the World War II era, officers patrolled during blackout conditions and received handcuffs, nightsticks, armbands, whistles, gloves, and helmets (first issue); the age limit was extended to 42 years old and height to five feet, eight inches. And increased youth truancy required another female officer, Mary Morrison, to assist Loretta R. Noonan. (Courtesy of the Cavanaugh family.)

Officers pictured in 1943 are, from left to right, (first row) John A. White, Patrick Sheehan, Walter O'Neil, and Sgt. Thomas Cavanaugh; (second row) Joseph Jullarine, Melvin Jetmore, John Crowley, and Royal Bitgood; (third row) Harold Goldberg, Jack "Tex" Heard, Arthur Feeley, and William Riordan. Bitgood and three other officers were bitten by a woman in 1953, which was reported by a Philadelphia newspaper. Bitgood retired as a detective. (Courtesy of retired Lt. William Lacey Jr.)

Seen here are examples of sidearms that New London police officers would use; from top to bottom are guns from 1915, 1925, and 1942. The desk sergeant would issue a gun to the supernumeraries, who had to supply their own bullets. At the end of their shifts, they would return the guns. (Courtesy of Chief Peter G. Reichard.)

An unidentified traffic booth police officer is shown on State Street at the corner of Bank Street in the 1940s. A second booth was located on State Street on the corner of Main Street. Eventually, cement bases were poured so there would be less damage to the traffic boxes when hit by vehicles. (Courtesy of retired Lt. William Lacey Jr.)

This is an example of a 1943 ticket belonging to officer James F. Sullivan. This ticket was handwritten for the violation of "Permitting rider on Running Board" at 5:55 p.m. on March 27, 1943. The dark-purple carbon paper went between the pages, and the top slip would be ripped out and given to a citizen. The left portion of the image displays the reverse side of what remains in the officer's booklet. This driver's plea entered was "N.G.," and the disposition was "G $10 Flat." The booklet was made by printers on Raymond Street, New London, Connecticut. (Courtesy of Dr. John Sullivan.)

This is a photograph of Bank and State Streets. This photograph was part of a handout by Universal Signal Company's secretary and treasurer P. L. Shea in New London, Connecticut, regarding the universal traffic signal. This would solve the problem of the trolley, cars, and pedestrians. The police officer could see the trolley approaching and switch the lights so the trolley could proceed and the cars and pedestrians would wait. The system "is electrically operated by lighted, colored, lettered signs, whereby the moving public can read in print and color the orders under which they can proceed." The traffic officer can manipulate four levers at the curb or from his position of elevation. At the base and to the left of the telephone pole is a police officer standing on a platform. The V-shaped objects overhead are the trolley wires. (Courtesy of Joan Corcoran McIntire.)

On August 16, 1945, crowds celebrate Victory over Japan Day (V-J Day). A police officer stands on the sidewalk watching a man on horseback at the crosswalk on the corner of State and Main Streets. From 1940 to 1945, about 3,500 townsmen served in World War II, with 59 killed. (Courtesy of the Public Library of New London.)

This photograph shows crowds gathered on August 16, 1945, to celebrate the surrender of Japan ending World War II. Seen to the right is a "cop in a box," as they were often referred to until 1952, when they were replaced with automatic lights. Note the concrete block the booth is built upon to protect the officer when vehicles hit it. (Courtesy of the Public Library of New London.)

This view of State Street looks west during the tercentenary parade on June 15, 1946. The movie *Renegades* is advertised on the Garde's marquee (far right), and the courthouse is at the top of the hill. Some estimates put the crowd at 20,000. (Courtesy of the Public Library of New London.)

Sgts. William Riordan (left) and Thomas L. Cavanaugh (right) are shown with a truck that was going to be the getaway vehicle during a botched robbery at Michael's Dairy in the early 1940s. Per the families of officers, the Buscetto family was one of many who allowed officers to get some rest out of the cold and rain during their shift. Cavanaugh was acting police chief in 1956. (Courtesy of Michael Buscetto Jr.)

Patrolman Charles Davidson walks the football field at Veterans Field on Cedar Grove Avenue in the 1940s. He would serve as chief of police from 1970 to 1973. (Courtesy of Renée Vogt.)

The chains on the left side of the photograph held whistles. The top chain is gold, and the bottom is silver; they were worn depending upon rank. To the top right is a pin with a "P," and beneath that is a State of Connecticut "three grape vines" button (worn generically by officers in the state), cuff links in the shape of handcuffs, and a key chain with a club. The whistle is called the Acme Thunderer and was made in England by GEMSCO. At times, the Boy Scout whistle (with the inscription "Be Prepared") might be substituted. (Courtesy of the retired Capt. Gordon Dickens family.)

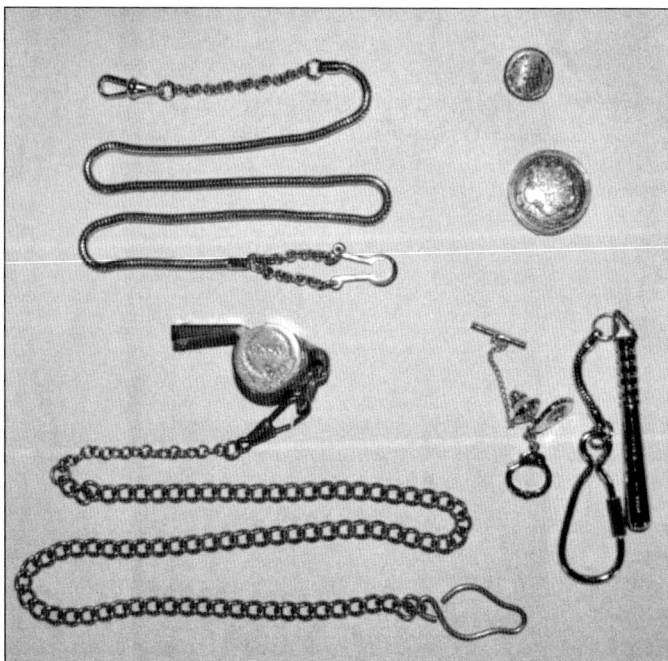

Capt. William T. Babcock led the department from 1933 to 1946. He was granted military leave of absence from the force. The designation of the title of chief and his retirement occurred while he was on military leave. Thus he retired with the title of chief of police. Earlier in his career, he served in the capacity of a motorcycle officer. On one of his patrols, he gave chase to criminals until reaching Salem. In 1943, an ordinance established a pension roll for the City of New London. (Courtesy of the New London Police Department.)

Chief John J. Courtney led the department from 1946 to 1961. During his tenure, supernumeraries had to take an examination, be residents of New London for at least three years, be between the ages of 21 and 30, and be at least five feet, nine inches tall, with weight proportionate to age and height. The list fluctuated from 14 to 35 men. In 1960, the eight county governments in the state ceased to exist after 294 years when the state took oversight. (Courtesy of the New London Police Department.)

The nightstick, or billy club, on the left is made of hardwood. Next is the .38 snub-nose handgun with a holster below it. Above the handgun is the .38 ammunition gun belt attachment. To the far right is the claw and the leather pouch it would sit in. The claw was used to grasp a wrist and tighten, rendering a person less likely to resist. All this equipment was carried by officers. (Courtesy of the New London Police Union.)

This sign was held by criminals to have their photograph taken at the station. It stopped being used sometime in the 1990s. In 1947, the state outlawed job discrimination through the Fair Employment Practices Act. In 1948, the station on North Bank Street was deeded to the Day Company.

Chappel Homestead (above), on the corner of Union Street and Federal Street, is seen in the 1900s. This house was replaced about 1922 by Stanton School (below), which became the police department in 1948. (Courtesy of the Public Library of New London.)

Operations began at this New London Police Department building on December 28, 1948, and continued until 1985. A police court was located on the second floor, police headquarters were on the first floor, and the prisoner holding cells were in the basement. Murals of a police theme decorated the interior. (Courtesy of the Public Library of New London.)

Boat Race Day celebrated the Yale-Harvard regatta with traffic officer Sgt. William J. Corcoran, shown on the Policeman's Benevolent Association float on Williams Street in June 1949. According to the *Day* newspaper, an estimated 30,000 viewers were along the parade route. Corcoran patrolled the hurricane of 1938. In the days following the hurricane, he transported children to school in a police cruiser when water was too high to walk through. In December 1941, the city council required shoeshine boys to register under "an Ordinance Providing for the Licensing of Bootblacks." To register as a bootblack, one had to be at least 14 years old, get permission from his school principal, and interview and then obtain a license from the chief of police. This ordinance remained until 2009. In 1941, there were 30,094 residents, with 47 percent American-born; 7,670 homes, with 35 percent owned by their occupants; and 76 policemen. In response to the attack on Pearl Harbor, the city council attempted to pass an ordinance to make all residents and anyone within city limits for more than 12 hours acquire a formal ID that would need to be shown upon request from police. (Courtesy of the Public Library of New London.)

Three

1950s

Officer Roger A. DuPont Sr., seen here, wears badge No. 17. He was known as "the motorcycle police officer" for almost two decades. The earlier police officers were rumored to have stuffed newspapers and cardboard inside their coats and up their sleeves in order to protect themselves from the chill of wind when they rode. In 1956, DuPont joined Louis C. Pine and served special duty with the detective bureau after safe-cracking robberies occurred in the city and surrounding towns. The next set of officers to ride motorcycles after DuPont would be in 1980. (Courtesy of Roger A. DuPont Jr.)

Police officers pose for a picture in the 1950s. During this decade, the *Norwich Bulletin* reported that "a female dog with puppies gave Patrolmen Edwin Harkins and William Murphy some trouble" as they investigated a theft at a home; the *Nautilus*, the first nuclear submarine, was commissioned; there was a crackdown on motorcycle noise; redevelopment of the city began; and in 1959, the US Navy Underwater Sound Laboratory employed 800 people, one of the largest area employers. (Courtesy of the Bruhns-Wells-Courtney family.)

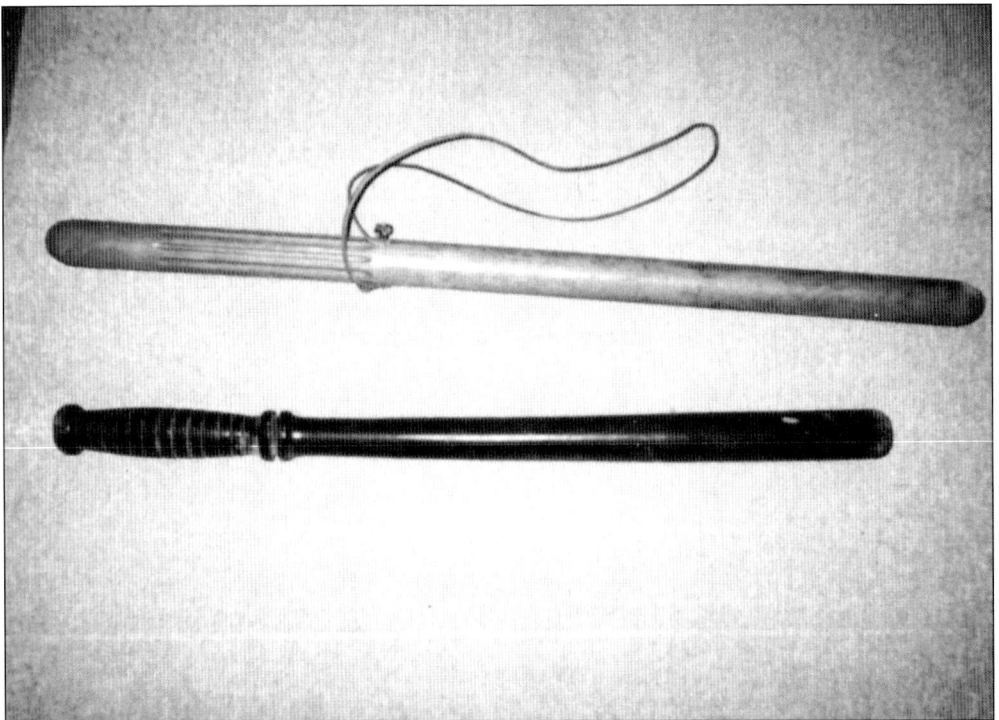

Wooden nightsticks made from hardwood were carried by officers from the 1800s through the 1980s. They were replaced by expandable metal batons that remained collapsed on the belt until needed. On October 11, 1952, the *Day* reported no arrests for four days; the same year, the city council refused to fund a female sergeant. In 1954, the police women's association began.

This is a page from Sergeant Murphy's monthly time book from December 15, 1957, to January 11, 1958. A page from 1965 noted that Sgt. J.A. White inspected guns and cuffs as part of regular checks. These books were still being used in 1967. (Courtesy of Sr. Sgt. Kevin McBride and the Paskewich family.)

The nightstick shown was referred to as a blackjack and was carried until the 1980s, when it was deemed too dangerous for modern-day less-lethal weapons. Modern deterrents are mace or pepper spray, bean bags shot from a modified barrel of a long gun, and stun guns that send an electric shock to the perpetrator. In 1893, the "humane police club" was displayed at the World's Fair by Dr. A.W. Nelson. It was shorter and made of hard rubber.

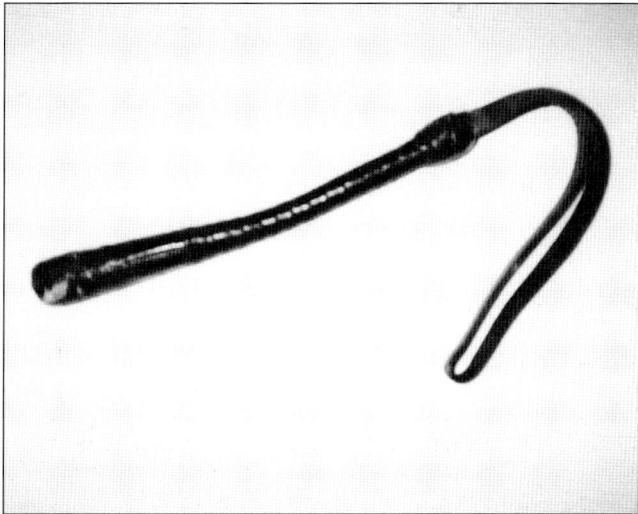

Patrolman James F. Sullivan stands at the top of State Street in June 1951. This was the main route for vehicles headed to Boston or New York. Note the row of cars parked facing into what would be Tony D's Restaurant and where cars must now parallel park. His son James "Jim" R. Sullivan served as a sheriff. (Photograph by Commercial Engraving Co.; courtesy of the Public Library of New London.)

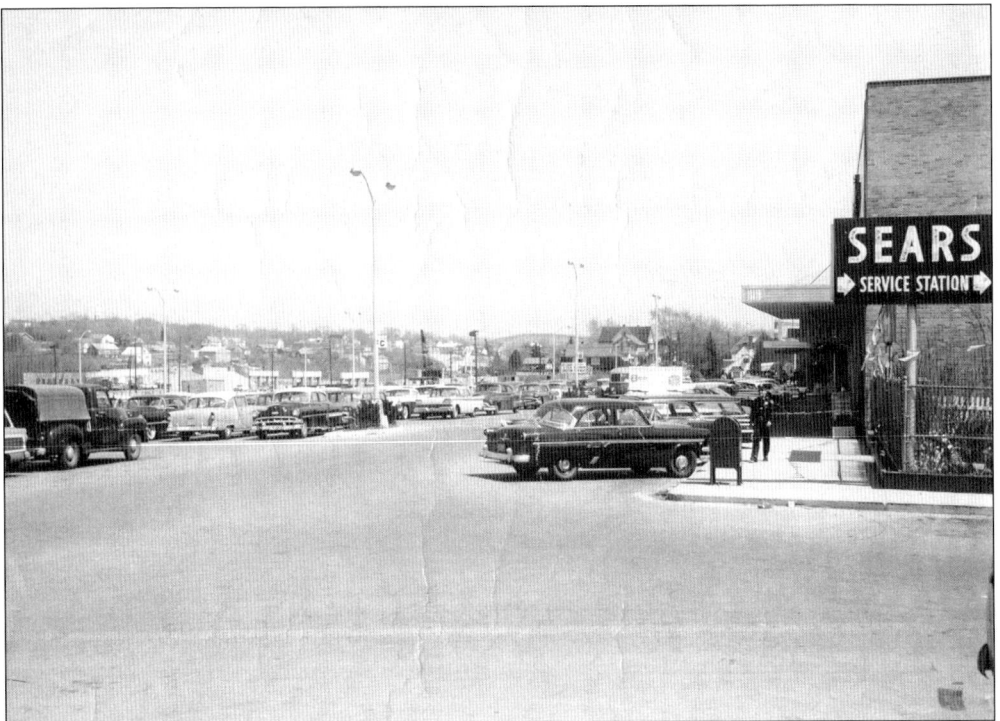

An officer is on patrol at the Sears store in the 1950s. Bradlees is behind the officer. To the left are columns that would become the Coleman Street overpass. Traffic lights were still controlling traffic driving east and west (what is now Interstate 95 North and South). (Courtesy of Sr. Sgt. Kevin McBride and the Paskewich family.)

This view from St. Bernard High School for Girls looks towards Williams Park. Officers direct traffic in the roundabout (placed in 1943) at Williams and Broad Streets, which was called Moses Square. Inside the park is a statue of Nathan Hale that was placed in 1935. (Courtesy of the Public Library of New London.)

A large crowd stands behind wooden barriers with police presence (both sergeants) at the railroad station. They await the 1953 New England basketball champions of New London High School. In 1951, Buckeley School had won; the team included Joseph Campagna, who would serve 21 years as an officer on the force. (Courtesy of the Public Library of New London.)

Capt. John W. Pearson is shown here with all badges from supernumerary to captain working for seven chiefs from 1952 to 1990. In April 1988, the 29-year police veteran was dragged by a car while trying to protect a fellow officer during an undercover sting. He recovered from his injuries to return to work but was no longer on the street. His injuries forced him to take an early retirement. (Courtesy of the retired Capt. John W. Pearson family.)

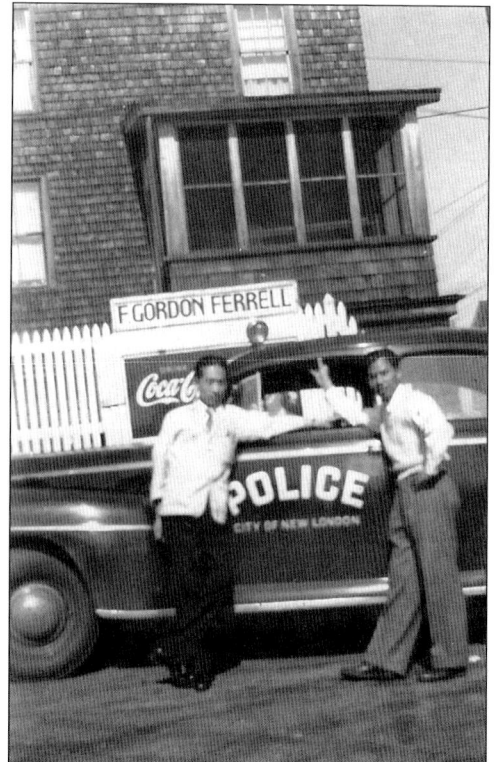

This was the police car style around the 1950s. Richard S.J. Wong is on the left, and an unidentified man is on the right. Under the ordinances of 1933 and 1942, officers were not allowed to walk or talk to each other or members of the community unless it was for official business. However, the Wong family, like other members of the public, welcomed officers into their restaurant. (Courtesy of George Wong.)

Officer Harry A. Chiappone Sr. is pictured in 1986. Beginning in the 1950s, he served with his brothers Joseph and Louis. He recalled a story of chasing a suspect from Bank Street through back alleys and over a fence. He says he looks back now and asks himself, "What was I thinking? The guy could have had a gun or a knife. But at the time, you just go." He is enjoying a safe retirement as of 2018. (Courtesy of Kenneth W. Edwards Jr.)

Cornelius "Con" Moriarty (center back) and Louis Pine (far right) are seen in this image. Pine is identified as chief on the back of this photograph; he served as a captain and a detective. During their time, the department shifted to 40-hour work weeks and days off on holidays. Council members had tried to pass an ordinance allowing employment at age 21 for supernumerary and age 25 for regular officer but had trouble agreeing. (Courtesy of Thomas Moriarty.)

Paul Hamler Sr. assists with the safe crossing of children at the corner of Broad Street and Connecticut Avenue in May 1951. Within six years, these kids would be able to visit animals at what would become Bates Woods Zoo, started by Officer Herbert Moran, who transferred to become a recreation director. (Courtesy of the Hamler family and the Connecticut Department of Education.)

The Knot Hole Gang was formed by generous sponsors and led by Officer Braxton W. Hill (see page 27) from about 1947 to 1954. He reserved 17 railroad cars for almost 1,300 children who were able to attend a professional baseball game each summer. As shown in this 1952 photograph, kids would march from Williams Street down State Street to board the train. (Courtesy of the Public Library of New London.)

Officer Joseph Salvatore Jullarine is shown around 1950. He would go on to be promoted to sergeant and was affectionately called "Sergeant Joe." He served for more than 30 years. His daughter Elaine would marry the son of police officer Cornelius Moriarty (below). Joe's nephews served on the force: brothers Harry (see page 51), Joseph, and Louis Chiappone. (Courtesy of Neil and Elaine Jullarine Moriarty.)

Officer Cornelius "Con" Moriarty (center) is seen with two unidentified men around 1950. He was heavily invested in the youth of the city and present for all of the dances that were popular at the time. He was one of the founders of the Policeman's Benevolent Association (PBA), a forerunner for the union. (Courtesy of Thomas Moriarty.)

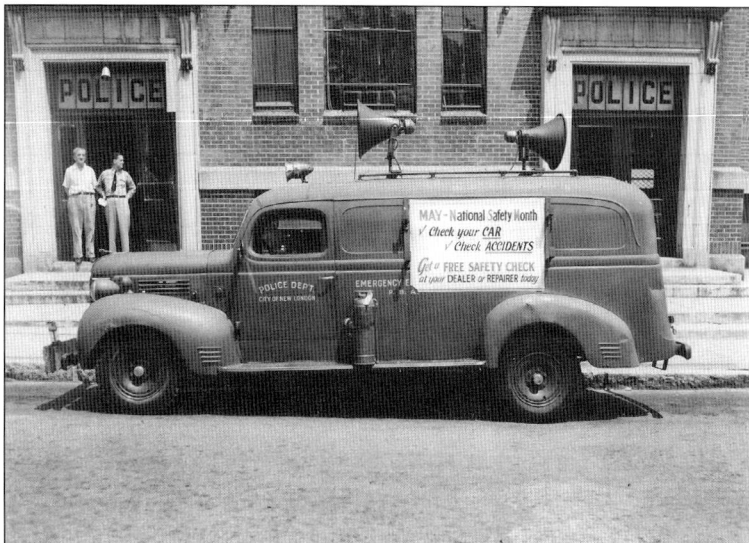

The New London Police Department "Speaker Truck" is pictured around 1957 in front of the police department at 111 Union Street. In 1959, there were 63 paid men, eight pieces of motor equipment, one power and sound truck, one station, and a three-way radio (valued at $60,000). (Courtesy of the New London Police Union.)

Patrolmen James F. Sullivan (left) and Donald Sloan (right) sort women's undergarments after the "panty thief" was apprehended in 1955. Sgt. William Riordan assisted with the investigation after several years of women's undergarments disappearing from clotheslines in backyards. Patrolman Sullivan caught the thief, or in slang terms, "made the collar." (Courtesy of Dr. John Sullivan.)

Sgt. Clarence "Pop" Wells is shown here at the desk of the police station at 111 Union Street in August 1953. Ten years prior, when he served as a detective, he and Sgt. Dennis W. Cavanaugh were complimented for catching thieves at the YMCA. Wells would go on to become a captain. His brother-in-law was Chief John J. Courtney (see page 41). (Photograph by CPO E.J. Parker; courtesy of the Bruhns-Wells-Courtney family.)

Seen here is a patch from Shore Patrol that was worn by military personnel who were assigned to patrol areas frequented by sailors. They assisted in keeping peace and were active through the 1980s, when this patch was still being worn. (Courtesy of the Bergeson family.)

2-46 (Rev. 7-15-58)

FBI NATIONAL ACADEMY

The course of training offered by the FBI National Academy will continue for a period of twelve weeks. You are advised that for a period of one hour each day during first ten weeks of the course of training, physical training will be provided and the following clothing is suggested:

1 pair of gym shoes	9.00
2 pairs white wool socks	2.00
1 pair gym trunks, preferably with elastic top	2.00
1 white gym shirt (optional)	2.00
1 pair locker room clogs, of either wooden or rubber construction	3.00
	2.00
1 athletic supporter	22.00
1 gray or white sweat shirt CHINOS	12.00
	34.00

A suitable locker will be provided for you in which to store this equipment. If it is not available in your home town, you may purchase same at a nominal cost upon your arrival in Washington.

The Bureau will provide, without cost, a .38 caliber revolver for your use in fire-arms training, or you may bring your own revolver if you care to do so. However, it should be borne in mind that the ammunition which will be furnished for firearms training, without cost, is available only in .38 and .45 caliber.

Civilian clothes are worn exclusively during the period of training, but you should arrange to bring along some fatigue or work clothing, which may be used from time to time on the outdoor range.

It is entirely likely that some of the officials of your own department or city, county or state administration will find occasion to be in Washington while you are taking this course of training. If so, I hope you will feel free to invite them to call at the Bureau while they are here and arrangements will be made for them to go on a tour of the facil-ities of the Federal Bureau of Investigation.

You will report for this course of training not later than 9:00 A.M. on the date designated, at Room 5256, Department of Justice Building, located between 9th and 10th Streets on Pennsylvania Avenue, N.W., Washington, D. C. Inquiries of the guards at the entrance of the building will enable you to obtain proper guidance to this office.

All sessions of the FBI National Academy are held in Washington except for one week of firearms training at the FBI Academy at Quantico, Virginia. Accordingly, it is necessary for those in attendance to obtain living quarters in the city of Washington. Living expenses vary depending upon the type of quarters selected. Generally speaking, however, living expenses in Washington are somewhat higher than in many smaller com-munities.

This is a list of items that attendees were expected to bring to the FBI academy for special training in 1959. Locally, in 1953, the *Norwich Bulletin* published an article about a prisoner marriage at the New London County Jail "in the living room of the quarters of deputy jailor Eric R. and Mrs. Swanson." The probation officer was the justice of the peace, and the city clerk issued a marriage license. The husband returned to jail and was awaiting bail money. In 1977, the department was reorganized to include a standardized roll call with inspections of a standardized uniform, a system to better track crime, a formal system for civilian complaints, promotion by merit exam, a youth bureau, a crime prevention and community relations program and formal in-service training, and numbered memo pads for routine police work and when officers needed to report to court for subpoenas. A new alarm system was set up to decrease the number of false alarms from merchants (2,120); crime on Bank Street decreased from 1976, which was not the public's perception; and the number of auxiliaries increased from 27 to 38. (Courtesy of Dr. John Sullivan.)

UNITED STATES DEPARTMENT OF JUSTICE

FEDERAL BUREAU OF INVESTIGATION

In Reply, Please Refer to
File No.

WASHINGTON 25, D. C.

February 18, 1959

Mr. James F. Sullivan
8 Grand Street
New London, Connecticut

Dear Mr. Sullivan:

Your letter of February 14, 1959, addressed to the Director of the FBI National Academy has been received. In answer to your request, we do have a number of recommended rooming houses and hotels where officers attending the FBI National Academy usually live. Instead of furnishing you with a list of these rooming houses and hotels it is suggested that you come to Room 5256, Department of Justice Building, upon your arrival in Washington, at which time assistance will be given to you in locating desirable living quarters.

We will be looking forward to having you with us at the next session of the National Academy.

Sincerely yours,

John Edgar Hoover
Director

Seen here is return correspondence in 1959 to Officer James F. Sullivan from the first director of the US Department of Justice's Federal Bureau of Investigation, J. Edgar Hoover. He remained director until 1972, when he died at the age of 77. (Courtesy of Dr. John Sullivan.)

In 1959, patrolman James F. Sullivan is shown practicing point shoulder shooting with a .38 caliber revolver at the Federal Bureau of Investigation ranges in Quantico, Virginia. He completed training with the 63rd session of the FBI National Academy. Prior to him, Capt. Clarence Wells had attended and graduated. (Courtesy of Dr. John Sullivan.)

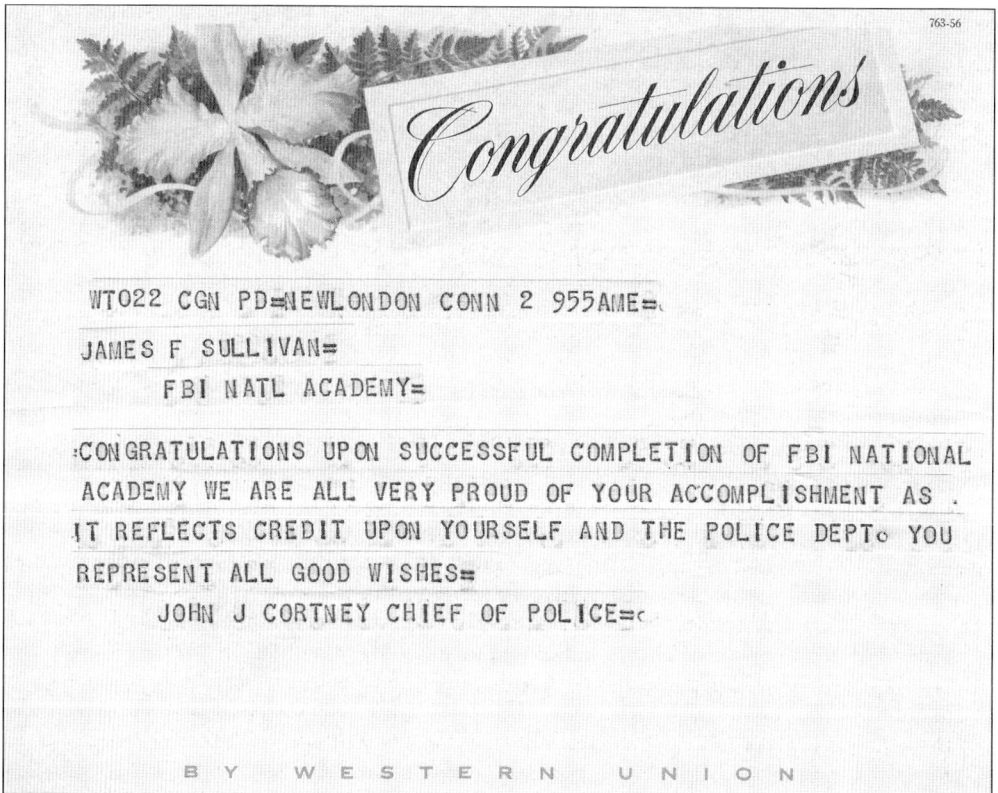

763-56

WT022 CGN PD=NEWLONDON CONN 2 955AME=

JAMES F SULLIVAN=
    FBI NATL ACADEMY=

:CONGRATULATIONS UPON SUCCESSFUL COMPLETION OF FBI NATIONAL
ACADEMY WE ARE ALL VERY PROUD OF YOUR ACCOMPLISHMENT AS .
IT REFLECTS CREDIT UPON YOURSELF AND THE POLICE DEPT. YOU
REPRESENT ALL GOOD WISHES=
    JOHN J CORTNEY CHIEF OF POLICE=

B Y   W E S T E R N   U N I O N

This is the telegram sent in 1959 by New London Police chief John J. Courtney to patrolman James F. Sullivan upon completion of his training at the FBI National Academy. Sullivan was expected to train other officers in the department on what he learned at the academy when he returned. (Courtesy Dr. John Sullivan.)

58

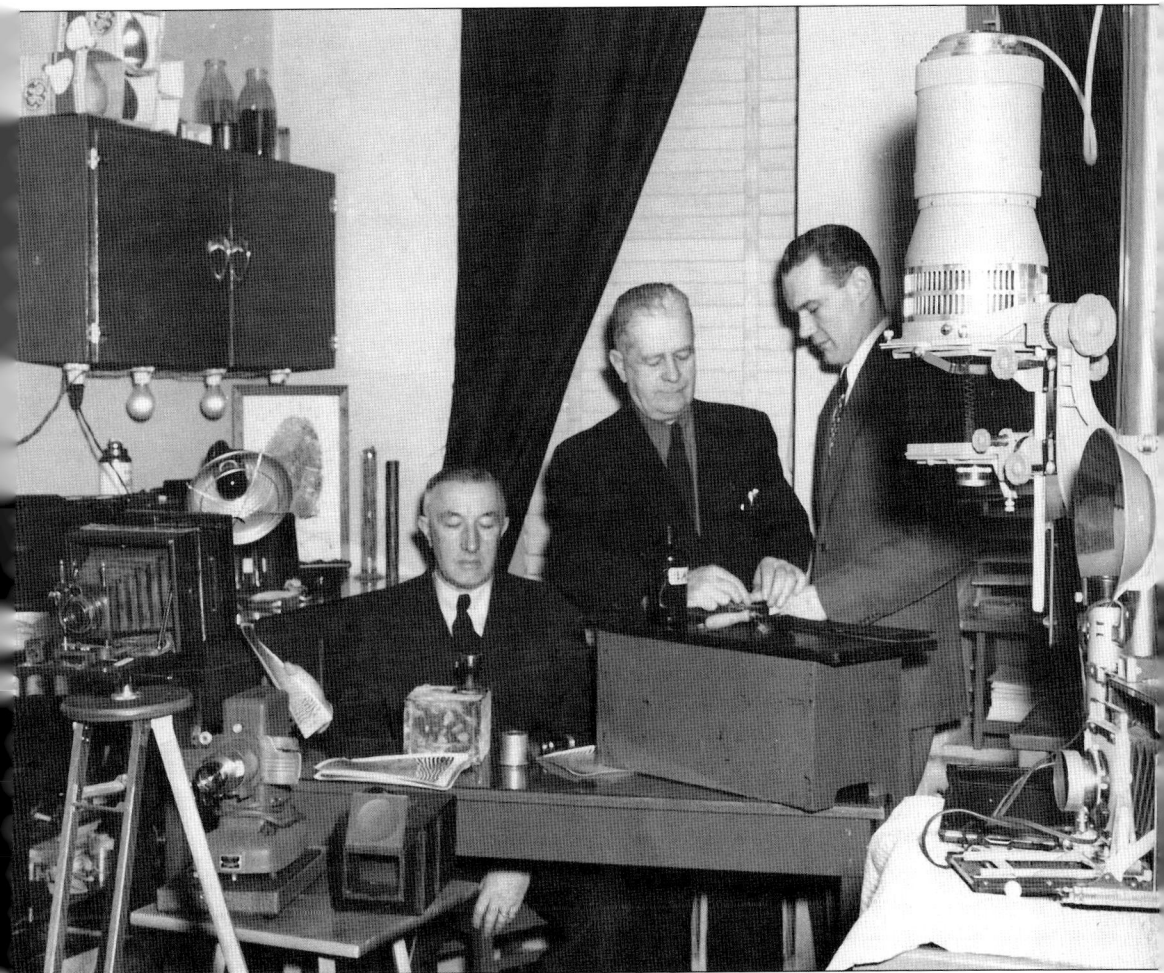

Det. Lt. Dennis W. Cavanaugh is shown seated in his work environment around 1955. He was appointed a supernumerary in 1918, became a regular policeman in 1919, was promoted to Grade A police officer in 1927, became sergeant in 1934, was promoted to detective sergeant in 1946, and was promoted to detective lieutenant in 1956. He refused promotion to captain because he wanted to remain with the detective bureau. He retired at the age of 65 after 38 years with a monthly pension. He passed away about five years after retirement, and his pension stopped as there were no provisions in place to provide for widows. His other talents were expressed as a member of the Old Timers Band in the Niagara Engine Company No. 1 Volunteer Fire Department playing the violin and banjo. In May 1937, Inside Detective magazine featured a case Sergeant Cavanaugh responded to after being summoned by special officer Charles Davidson. A woman had been found down after "falling" out of a plate-glass window of the Danceland Casino near Ocean Beach. A bandleader was charged with causing her death. Additional officers involved were Patrick Sheehan and George Laboue. The case against the orchestra leader was dismissed by three judges based on eye-witness testimony. (Courtesy of Joel F. Riley.)

Officer Richard R. Brown is pictured in 1957. His son William F. Brown (below) would go on to serve on the force. Note the difference in weapons and no whistle. Additionally, more cars were available for patrol in later years. (Courtesy of the Sgt. William F. Brown family.)

Officer William F. Brown, son of Officer Richard R. Brown, stands near the patrol car that was the style around the 1980s. He is parked in front of the Union Street building. A light bar on the roof of his car held two lights and a speaker. The windows were of the manual style. (Courtesy of the Sgt. William F. Brown family.)

Four

1960s–2018

Sgt. Victor Johnson (left), a US Army veteran, joined the force in 1954 as a supernumerary and was hired full-time in 1961. Johnson retired 32 years later as a sergeant. Theodore "Ted" Kovalik (not shown) shared his locker with Johnson because he did not have one assigned to him when he was first hired. Johnson was a charter member of the New London National Association for the Advancement of Colored People (NAACP). Lt. Gordon Dickens (right) started on foot patrols, went to school at the University of New Haven to earn his associate's degree, raised a family, and walked a picket line for better wages. Dickens retired as a captain. The PBA in essence formalized as the union, now known as AFSCME CT 724. (Photograph by Sgt. William F. Brown.)

This booklet is sponsored

as a community service

by

The

SAVINGS BANK

of New London

63 MAIN STREET

SHOPPING CENTER BRANCH

New London Bridge Approach

Member Federal Deposit Insurance Corporation

GUARDIANS

of your
Property and Welfare

NEW LONDON
POLICE

CALL GI 3-4315

This 18-page booklet held information that would help citizens not become victims. They could call the department via phone number GI 3-4315. The holes were placed so this handout could be hung near the home telephone around 1961. In 2018, there are a variety of ways of communicating with police. Citizens can walk into headquarters or call the main number (860-447-5269) via landline or cell phone. Emergency 911 is a centralized system tracking where the call or text is coming from. Citizens are encouraged to "Be Crime Stoppers" via the department's website, which reads, "Help Fight Crime & Partner-up with NLPD! All tips are confidential and anonymous. Download the app for your Android or iPhone (NLPDTip): Text NLPDTip + your tip to Tip411 (847411)." The department has a Facebook page (www.facebook.com/NewLondonPolice) and sends tweets from a Twitter account (@NLPDCT). Loudspeakers are still used to announce bans for parking, such as during snow removal. (Both, courtesy of the Bruhns-Wells-Courtney family.)

Officer Theodore "Ted" Kovalik is the man handing the girl a soda in June 1962 during PBA Day at the beach. The child is being held by Officer Richard R. Brown. Children are identified on the back of the photograph as Teresa, Kathy, Rosanne, and Kathy, Earl, and Soupre Pearson. Kovalik responded to the hurricane of 1938 as a supernumerary and retired 39 years later in 1977 as a lieutenant. (Courtesy of the Sgt. William F. Brown family.)

Sgt. Joseph "Sergeant Joe" Jullarine serves ice cream to youth at Ocean Beach Park as provided through the PBA during the 1950s and 1960s. The PBA was formerly known as the Police Athletic League (PAL). (Courtesy of Neil and Elaine Jullarine Moriarty.)

BEAT ASSIGNMENTS AUGUST 20 - SEPTEMBER 16, 1961

7:30 A.M. - 4:00 P.M.		3:30 P.M. - 12:00 M		11:30 P.M. - 8:00 A.	
DESK: Sgt. Elwood		DESK: Sgt. Sullivan		DESK: Sgt. Goldberg	
STREET: Sgt. Feeley		STREET: Sgt.W.Murphy		STREET: Sgt.J.A.Whit	
Beat No.		Beat No.		Beat No.	
Hdqr.	K.Bucko	Hdqr.	Jetmore	Hdqr.	McIninch
1.	Petchark	1.	Shea	1.	V. Johnson
2.	P.Cavanagh	2.	Donahue	2.	Gennotti
3.	Campagna	3.	Northrop	3.	J. Sheehan
4.	J.Cavanagh	4.	Jullarine	4.	Leo Kovalik
4A.	Chiappone *	4A.	J.Paskewich **	4A.	
5.	Gardner	5.	Grillo	5.	Clark
6.	J.E.White	6.	Fazzina	6.	F.Paskewich
7.	D.Sheehan	7.	Vincent	7.	R. Johnson
8.		8.	J. Paskewich **	8.	Popa
9.	Kurpiewski	9.	Mullen	9.	Eisenstein
#	Egger	#	Crowley	#	Rafferty
	D.Murphy		Bitgood		T.Kovalik
	Trafaconda		Street		Brown
	J.Pearson		Heard		C.Bucko
	E.Pearson		Mugovero		Miceli
					Murach

SPECIAL ASSIGNMENT: - DuPont - Motorcycle Duty
Sloan - To Ocean Beach Park

* On the 7:30 A.M. Squad Beat No. 8 is left vacant and the man originally
assigned to this Beat is assigned to Beat No. 4-A (See revised Beat
Assignments for location of Beat No. 4-A). Men assigned to Beat No. 9
will also cover Beat No. 8.

** On the 3:30 P.M. Squad the men assigned to Beat No. 4-A will remain on
this Beat until 9:00 P.M. at which time he will take over Beat No. 8.
The man assigned to Beat No. 4 will also cover No. 4-A after 9:00 P.M.
Up until 9:00 P.M. the man assigned to Beat No. 9 will also cover Beat
No. 8.

NOTICE: There will be strict enforcement of the Motor Vehicle Laws and all
members of the Department will be held responsible especially men assigned
to Motor Patrol. Strict enforcement of the Parking Meter and Traffic Ordinances will also be carried out. PARKING OVERNIGHT IN BUSINESS DISTRICT
IS PERMITTED DURING THE PERIOD APRIL 1ST TO NOVEMBER 1ST.
    ATTENTION MEN ASSIGNED MOTOR PATROL: - Motor Patrol is under supervision
of Traffic Sergeant Corcoran. Any defective cars or equipment should be
called to Sgt. Corcoran's attention.
    Men filling vacancies will be assigned to Motor Patrol Duty on the
basis of ability and performance of duty, not seniority.

jm

This is an example of assignments typed by Sgt. John J. Murphy in 1961. Originally stapled to this page was a type-written list of days off for a four-week period. In 1962, the *Norwich Bulletin* reported that Sgt. J.A. White, listed on nights (and father of five), was shot three times with .25-caliber bullets in an "11-shot exchange" after White pulled a car over. He was transported via taxi to recover at Lawrence & Memorial Hospital. In 1962, the *Day* reported that a police car siren jammed and could not be shut off. In 1963, auxiliary police captain Herman Goss assisted with water patrols, which were usually conducted by John T. "Tex" Heard, who used his own boat at times. This era saw race riots and anti–Vietnam War protests, the assassinations of Pres. John F. Kennedy and Dr. Martin Luther King Jr., the redistricting of voting areas, Medicare coverage, the first human heart transplant, and the first man on the moon. (Courtesy of Sr. Sgt. Kevin McBride and the Paskewich family.)

This is an image of the police department at 111 Union Street in 1962. Patricia H. McCarthy (seated fourth from left) started in October 1957 after Loretta R. Noonan retired in August 1957. McCarthy, a nurse, was deemed more mature than the other five candidates who were under the age of 30. The other women were offered the opportunity to be supernumeraries. (Courtesy of retired Det. Gerard J. Gaynor Jr.)

Seen here is an example of tickets issued in 1966. Local character-citizen "Cowboy" was issued a ticket for intoxication, which was "Nolled." Cowboy was born in New London in 1899. He was a contender in local boxing rings after the end of World War I and was a retired ironworker. Officers would "arrest" him during inclement weather to provide shelter and food. A year after this ticket was issued, Cowboy died. He was 68 years old.

Francis P. O'Grady was chief from 1961 to 1970. In 1961, the police headquarters was at 111 Union Street. The walking beats and cars were about equal at four and four. By 1970, there were more patrol cars on the road than walking beats and, on some shifts, only patrol cars. The district courts were in place, and there were no more local justice courts. (Courtesy of the New London Police Department.)

Patrolman Frank Paskewich stands next to a 1906 statue in the likeness of John Winthrop Jr. during a celebration day of history in New London in the 1960s. This area is where the town's original jail was located. In 1966, Paskewich went to radar school, followed by Officer Joseph Mugovero, who ran radar a year later. In 1972, Paskewich was appointed coordinator of the diving squad. (Courtesy of Sr. Sgt. Kevin McBride and the Paskewich family.)

Sgt. Neil Donahue, shown around 1967 inside the 111 Union Street station, served from November 1946 to August 1980. He was a relative of the Cavanaugh family. (Courtesy of the New London Police Union.)

Pictured in 1968, from left to right, are (first row) Sgt. John H. Egger, John Grillo, Robert Perry, Harry Chiappone, Harold Vincent, Nuell Northrop, and Sgt. Joseph Jullarine; (second row) William "Bill" Murphy, Joseph Mugovero, George Peabody, Richard West, and Joseph "Jeff" Watterson Jr. Watterson joined the force after serving as a Marine and later tranferred to and retired from the Waterford Police Department. Missing from the photograph are Ray Burke, Eugene and Russell Cavanaugh, Art Davis, Carmelo Fazzina, David Jetmore, Gerald Maranda, Donald Sloan, and John "Jack" Weinberg. (Courtesy of the New London Police Union.)

No. 1 patrolman Patrick Sheehan is shown in the 1950s. His sons, Eugene, Patrick, and Dennis, joined him on the police force. When he joined the force as a supernumerary in 1920 (see page 20), it had a patrol wagon, horse, harness, and equipment, which were kept at the police station all the time for the use of transporting prisoners. Prior to that, officers shared equipment with other city departments, causing a delay in prisoner transports. In the mid-1920s, most arrests were for intoxication and violation of traffic laws. (Courtesy of the John, Dennis, and Eugene Sheehan families.)

Officer Eugene "Gene" Sheehan, shown wearing badge No. 48, was one of three sons of officer Patrick Sheehan. In the early 1950s, women's names were showing up on the rolls of supernumeraries: Patricia Hullivan, Mary E. Smith, Barbara A. Cavanaugh, and Lorraine K. Homola. (Courtesy of the John, Dennis, and Eugene Sheehan families.)

A corporal since 1973, Dennis F. "Denny" Sheehan is shown in his 24th year in 1980 wearing No. 1 (also worn by his father, Patrick). In November 1949, he started as a supernumerary in a class with two African American residents, William J. Goode and Maurice J. Yates. As a patrolman, Sheehan and Salvatore Trafaconda used a resident's rowboat to save a boxer dog from the Thames River. (Courtesy of the John, Dennis, and Eugene Sheehan families.)

Cpl. John Patrick Sheehan is shown at the Union Street police station in 1978. He and his brothers, Denny and Gene, followed in the footsteps of their father, Patrick (see pages 20 and 68). Dennis and John Patrick were appointed and promoted to corporal on the same day in January 1973. In 1973, a corporal made a base pay of approximately $10,000 per year. (Courtesy of the John, Dennis, and Eugene Sheehan families.)

In 1973, all officers pictured were sworn in as corporals. From left to right are (first row) Ernest Gardner, John Grillo, Frank Paskewich, Chief Charles G. Davidson, Carmelo Fazzina, Richard R. Brown, and John E. White; (second row) Frank Gennotti, Richard Johnson, Dennis Sheehan, John Patrick Sheehan, Donald Sloan, and Harold Vincent. Chief Davidson led the department from 1970 to 1973. (Courtesy of Sr. Sgt. Kevin McBride and the Paskewich family.)

Pictured from left to right around 1960 are (first row) Richard R. Brown, Richard Johnson, John Patrick Sheehan, Frank Paskewich, William Murach, Charlie Bucko (retired as a detective), and Lt. John White; (second row) William "Pat" Murphy, Ed Harkins, Frank Gennotti, John Miceli, and Tom Clark. (Courtesy of the Sgt. William F. Brown family.)

Chief John Crowley led the department from 1973 to 1977. In 1977, the department responded to almost 30,000 calls (approximately 560 per week). There was an increase in motor vehicle accidents, and 60 percent of housing in the city was rental property. Before caller ID and cell phones, a familiar directive given to family members by off-duty officers was "don't answer the phone." If the phone was answered, the officer could be ordered in to work. (Courtesy of the New London Police Department.)

Clayton Sizer, shown on patrol, began his career in 1972 as a supernumerary and was hired permanently in 1973 after serving two tours as an Army soldier in Vietnam. The second tour was to keep one of his brothers from having to deploy. Clayton retired from the New London Police Department in October 2002. His brother DeWitt "Al" Albert Sizer passed away after he retired from the police force and was a Navy foreign war veteran. (Courtesy of Michael Cavanaugh.)

Cpl. Ronald Cavanaugh, shown in the 1980s, is a second-generation officer, following his father, Jack (see page 34). His brother Eugene Russell "Russ" Cavanaugh, with whom he served, is shown at left. Ronald's son Michael retired from the force. (Courtesy of the Cavanaugh family.)

Second-generation Cpl. Eugene "Russ" Cavanaugh is shown around the 1980s. He served with his brother Ronald. In 1962, Russ began work as a police officer. In 1965, he was elected president of the Policeman's Benevolent Association. He was promoted to corporal in 1974 and retired in 1993. His son Russell is currently serving on the force. (Photograph by Sgt. William F. Brown.)

Third-generation Officer Michael Cavanaugh is shown standing in front and in line at roll call in the 1980s. He retired as a master patrol officer after 32 years on the force in June 2015. He served in the US Army and retired from the Connecticut Army National Guard. He is now working with at-risk youth. (Courtesy of Les Smith Jr.)

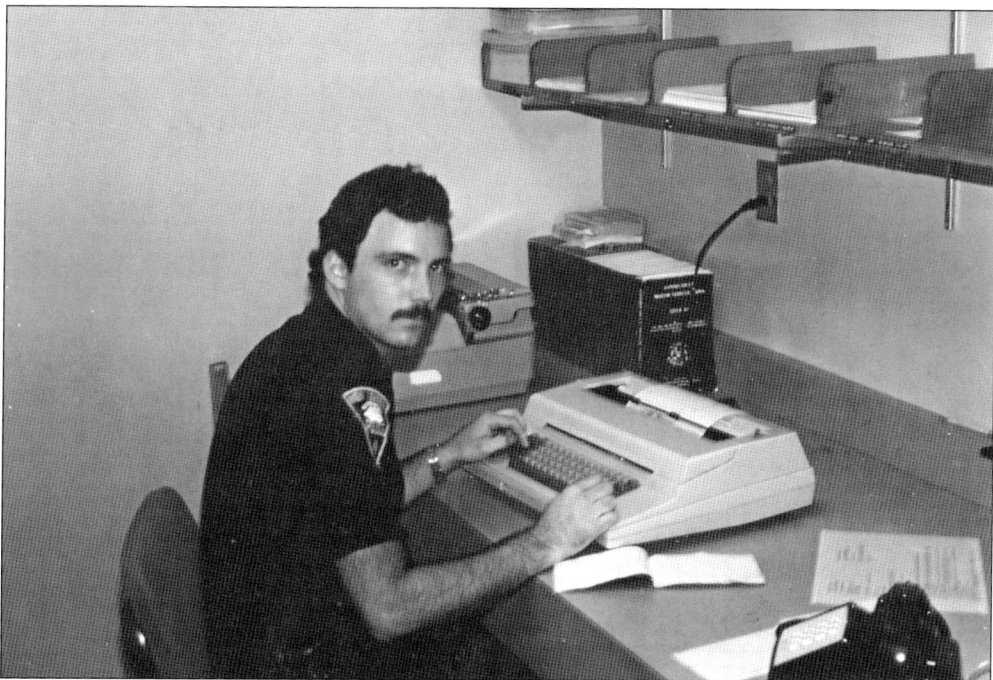

Third-generation patrolman Russell "Rusty" Cavanaugh sits in front of a typewriter around the 1980s. Rows of paperwork neatly stacked above his head would be used for reports. He began with the department as a supernumerary in 1985 and has risen to the rank of senior sergeant of the modern force using computers. (Courtesy of the New London Police Union.)

Pictured from left to right around the 1970s are city clerk Clark van der Lyke and Officers David Berry, Gary Brown, Richard Grohocki, and William F. Brown. (Courtesy of the Sgt. William F. Brown family.)

This c. 1960s–1970s view of South Water Street faces west and the rear of buildings on Bank Street with Amtrak tracks. The railroad station is to the right (not visible). Construction started on the Gold Star Memorial Bridge's second span in 1969, and redevelopment brought about many changes in the layout of the city during this time. (Courtesy of the Public Library of New London.)

Edward W. "Eddie" Paul, pictured in 2018, served as the mechanic for the police vehicles in the 1950s and 1960s. He transferred to the water department and was caretaker of millions of gallons of water citizens used as provided by Lake Konomoc. He retired after 54 years of service to the City of New London.

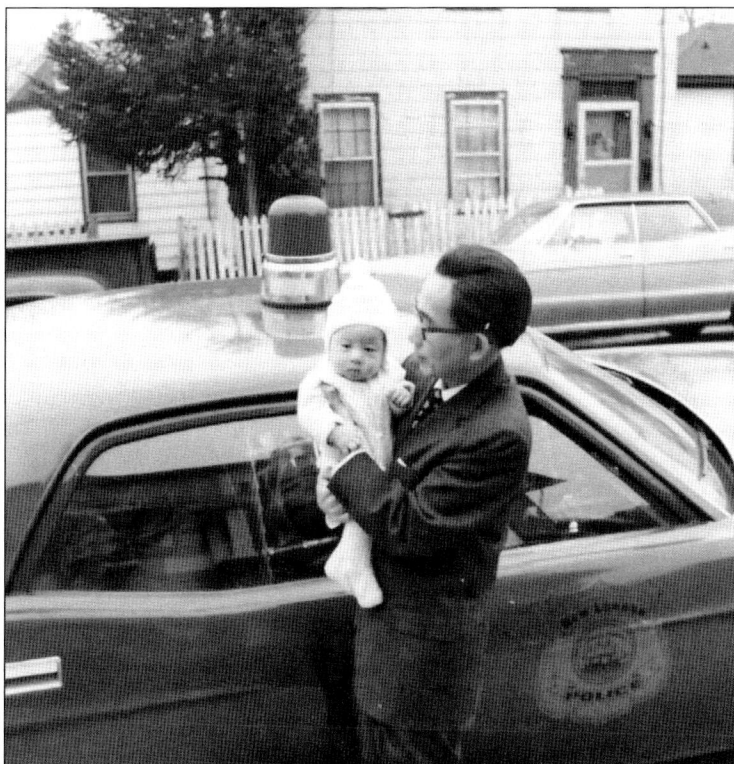

Steven Yu is the infant held by Richard S.J. Wong, a restaurant owner, as they stand in front of a police car around 1972. Officers continued to be welcomed by citizens and business owners. The cars were painted green and some crosswalks (downtown) were painted green under Chief John Crowley. In the late 1970s, the cruisers would evolve into blue with a white stripe and a large light bar across the roof. (Courtesy of George Wong.)

Standing from left to right around 1974 are Officers William D. Dittman Sr., Glen Davis, and Michael Guilfoil; kneeling is Clayton Sizer. They were conducting SWAT exercises at the Rhode Island National Guard camp. (Courtesy of the Sgt. William F. Brown family.)

David Berry joined the force in June 1967 and is shown here early in his career. He passed away in June 2002 (off duty). In 1978, a federal grant allowed for the installation of a new communications system so that 15 local and state law enforcement agencies were linked on a common emergency frequency. (Courtesy of the New London Police Department.)

Frank Paskewich stands next to a machine that recorded all the calls to the police department in the 1970s. The tapes had to be changed twice a day. In 1974, he was a detective, was in charge of operations, and was promoted to captain with a salary of $15,300. He was honored as Policeman of the Year by the Murphy Rathbun Post 189, Veterans of Foreign Wars. (Courtesy of Sr. Sgt. Kevin McBride and the Paskewich family.)

State Street is seen as it appeared from 1974 to 1990, when it was without vehicular traffic and was called Captains Walk. In 1976, there were no funds in the police budget to run a patrol boat. There were increased patrols on Bank Street and formalized training to interact with the youth. In 1974, the first female governor in the country elected on her own merits was Ella Grasso. (Photograph by Jack Urwiller; courtesy of the Public Library of New London.)

In this c. 1980s photograph, from left to right are (first row) Odd Krogrud (Vietnam veteran), John White, John Patrick Sheehan, Richard Johnson, and David Jetmore; (second row) Donald Sloan (chief 1981–1987), Bruce Rinehart (chief 1993–2009), Robert Perry, Theodore Kovalik, Charles "Jack" Alloway, Victor Johnson, John Manavas, and Charlie Bucko. (Courtesy of the Riordan-Manavas-Lewis families.)

Chief Richard Kistner served from 1987 to 1993. Upon his retirement, he wrote a letter to the editor of the Day praising key officers in the department who worked hard for police and community improvements. (Courtesy of the New London Police Department.)

In 1983, Chief Donald Sloan (left) is shown promoting John Pearson (center) and Frank Jarvis (right). Jarvis served in the US Navy and spent most of his career as a detective. This year, the legal drinking age was raised to 21 from 19. (Courtesy of the retired Capt. John W. Pearson family.)

Margaret "Peg" Ackley is shown as a patrol officer around the 1980s. Ackley would spend 30 years with the force, including special assignments to work with surrounding departments. She would be picked by the city manager to serve as chief for the final seven years of her career. (Courtesy of Kenneth W. Edwards Jr.)

Patrolman Ron Martel is pictured around the 1980s. He retired in April 2000 due to an injury. An additional skill he held was his ability to speak Spanish, which is valuable in emergency situations for the police and citizens. During this time, the traffic division installed new street signs, added bicycle lanes, and repainted pedestrian and vehicle lines. (Courtesy of Kenneth W. Edwards Jr.)

Sgt. Rocco Musorofiti sits with an early desktop computer and stacks of papers and reports around him. In front of him is a stand with a clip that held paperwork to view when typing. He served as a liaison to the court near the end of his career. (Courtesy of Kenneth W. Edwards Jr.)

Pictured in the 1970s are, from left to right, policewoman Loretta Brown, William F. Corcoran, and clerk Theresa Kin. The city wanted to consolidate records because of duplication of work. Lt. Edwin S. Harkins maintained records for traffic and desk officers, and Lt. John A. White maintained files for operations. Corcoran maintained the detective division files. Corcoran, the third generation in his family employed by the department (also shown on page 79), was nearing his retirement. (Courtesy of Joan Corcoran McIntire.)

Policewoman Loretta Brown and her husband, patrolman and detective T.K. Brown, are seen around 1980. Both had arresting powers, but T.K. is carrying a weapon with bullets. In 1978, the policewoman's duties fell under the Training and Communications Relations Unit. Her responsibilities included dealing with problems of child abuse, child neglect, family violence, and sex crimes. She proudly retained the title of policewoman until the end of her career in the 1990s. T.K. served in the US Coast Guard. (Courtesy of Les Smith Jr.)

TOTALPHONE could help!

For three years, Police Officer Rod Gaynor, Jr. has been the Crime Prevention Officer for the City of New London. He wrote us about how effective SNET's Totalphone® Service is as a crime prevention tool. We've been telling customers that for years.

"Your company has a product that I feel is an outstanding burglary prevention tool," he said. "Totalphone allows a person to forward calls to a location where someone can answer."

"We have found," Officer Gaynor explained, "that a burglar will select a victim by continued calls to determine when a family is not at home. In a burglary in New London, a woman lost $10,000 worth of silver while away on vacation." He said that, during their investigation, the police spoke with neighbors who reported getting a number of suspicious calls that week. "I believe that the victim was selected because she was unable to answer her phone."

EASY TO USE

It's simple to use Totalphone Service's "Call Forwarding" feature: By dialing a short code, your phone can be programmed to ring at another location. The person calling you has no way of knowing that you're not in your own living room.

Totalphone Service has other features: "Speed Calling" lets you reach frequently called numbers by dialing just one or two digits; with "Three-Way Calling" you can talk with people in two different locations; and "Call Waiting" lets you put one call on hold while answering a second.

About 2/3 of our customers can now have Totalphone, and we anticipate that by 1988, over 90% will be able to enjoy the service. In some

(con't.)

* Registered Trademark in Connecticut

S NEIGHBORHOOD PARTICIPATES IN NEIGHBORHOOD WATCH

👁 + 📞 = POLICE RESPONSE

Officer Gerard J. Gaynor Jr. is shown on a 1981 handout to assist the public with crime prevention. This brochure was made by Southern New England Telephone (SNET) in October 1981. It was edited by Mark Schannon, and the artist was Joe Meccariello. It was printed on recycled paper. (Courtesy of retired Det. Gerard J. Gaynor Jr.)

From left to right are Capt. Frank M. Paskewich, Sgt. Carmelo S. Fazzina, Sgt. John Pearson, Cpl. Joseph Mugovero, and Chief Samuel Fandel. Fandel served as chief from 1977 to 1981. (Courtesy of the retired Capt. John W. Pearson family.)

Pictured from left to right are Sgts. Sam Grillo, Jack Weinberg, and Gordon Dickens looking down the stairs outside the existing police station at 5 Governor Winthrop Boulevard around the 1980s. (Courtesy of Les Smith Jr.)

Patrolman William Pero started his career in October 1985 when he was sworn in as a supernumerary with Russell Cavanaugh, Michael Hedge, Jeffrey Kalolo, and Garry Sloan. They were regulars within days, completed brief classroom training, and were sent on foot patrol for a year followed by formal training at the academy. There were no field training officers (FTOs)—they were trained by their sergeants. (Courtesy of Kenneth W. Edwards Jr.)

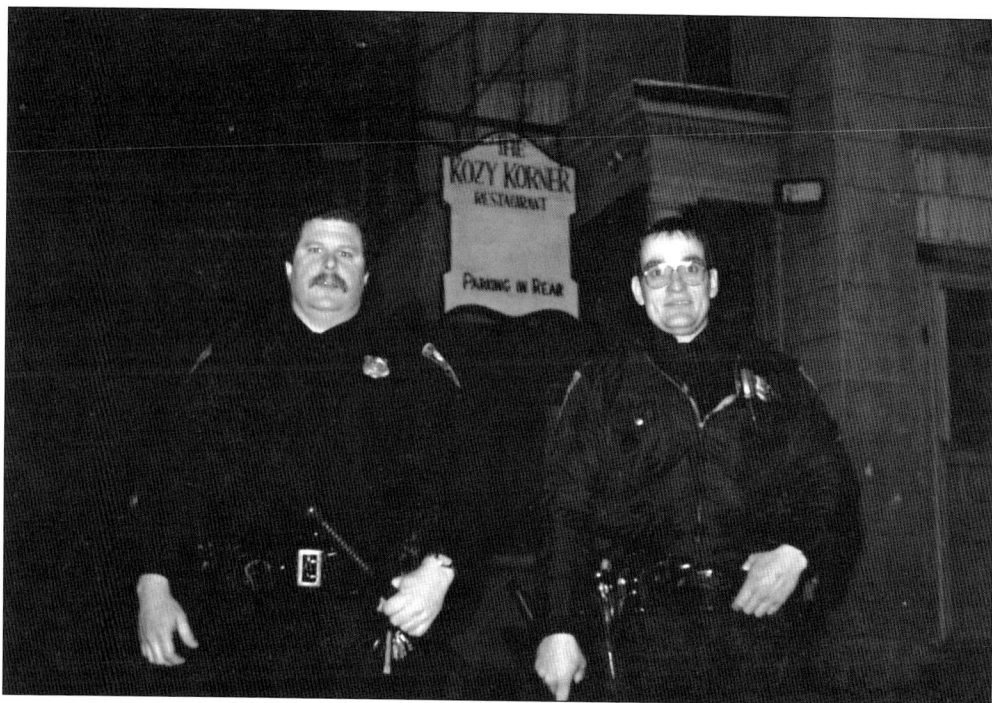

Officers Chris Miller (left) and Graham Mugovero pose with the Kozy Korner sign behind them while walking patrol on Truman Street. Miller held a record for bench press weight lifting. He retired as a detective. Mugovero retired in 2010 after 29 years on the force. (Courtesy of retired Lt. William Lacey Jr.)

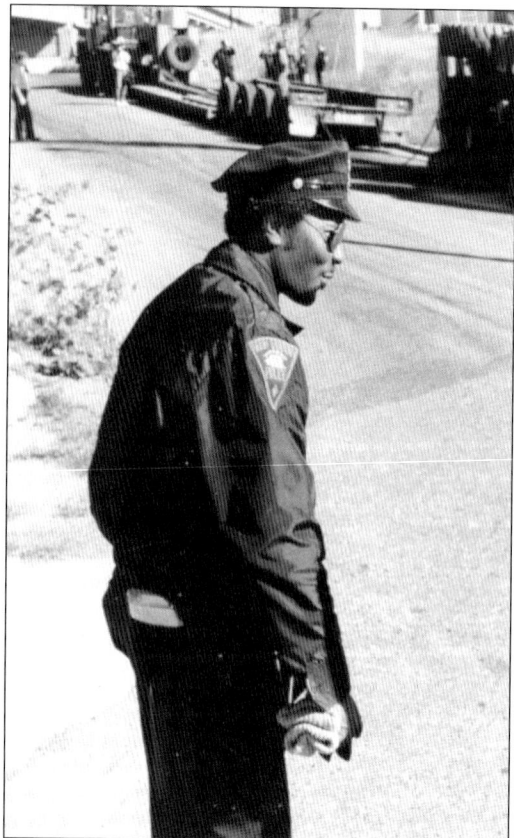

Officer Glenn Davis is shown near heavy equipment that is lying on its side on a street near the base of the support columns for the new, second Gold Star Memorial Bridge in the 1980s. (Courtesy of Les Smith Jr.)

Officers seen around 1968 are, from left to right, (first row) Richard R. Brown, John Manavas, Frank Gennotti, Richard Donovan, Sgt. Theodore Kovalik, John Patrick Sheehan, Frank Paskewich, Richard "Dick" Johnson, and William F. Brown (son of Richard R. Brown); (second row) Raymond Cramer, John Pearson, Leo Kovalik (Theodore's nephew), Charles Bucko, Paul W. Sawicki Jr., Victor Johnson, and Charles "Jack" Alloway. Missing from the photograph is William J. Kurpiewski. (Courtesy of the Sawicki family.)

Paul W. Sawicki III (left) and Axel Bergeson are pictured at Ocean Beach Park in 1984. (Paul's father is pictured above.) They both carry a pistol and a wooden nightstick. The beach draws in crowds upwards of 10,000 each summer, providing an Olympic-size swimming pool, gym, children's pool/play area, miniature golf, white-sand beach, picnic area, snacks, bar, and banquet hall. (Courtesy of the Bergeson family.)

Officer Russ DiNoto, at the Fishers Island Ferry slip near the Amtrak train station, is shown wearing a bicycle uniform. Wooden barricades (seen on the right) help keep vehicular and pedestrian traffic separate. Like many officers past and present, DiNoto is a member of the Benevolent and Protective Order of Elks (BPOE) No. 360. They have provided funding to the department for the dive team and the canines (K-9s). DiNoto served in the US Marine Corps. (Courtesy of the New London Police Union.)

This Dodge pickup truck and police boat in the 1990s were part of a display open to the public in a parking lot on North Frontage Road. Paul W. Sawicki III, Axel Bergeson, and Gordon Dickens were part of a handful of officers who trained in the 1970s on the Emergency Diving Squad, with test dives into waters off Dominion Millstone Power Stations in Waterford. (Courtesy of Kenneth W. Edwards Jr.)

Now-retired Officer Walter Morency is pictured in the late 1980s. At the end of a shift as a supernumerary, he was shot. Dispatchers did not hear his calls for assistance due to poor radio connectivity from his location on South Water Street. His calls for backup were heard by Officer William D. Dittman Sr., who was on patrol at Ocean Beach. Dittman was able to contact headquarters for help. (Courtesy of retired Lt. William Lacey Jr.)

Master Patrol Officer (MPO) James "Jimmy" Suarez is shown standing next to his patrol car, No. 54. Earlier in his career, he was shot multiple times. Prior to the shooting, he used to run with marathoner John J. Kelley. Sgt. J.A. White recommended him for the American Police Hall of Fame Legion of Honor, which Suarez received on December 16, 1991. White received a similar award (see page 64).

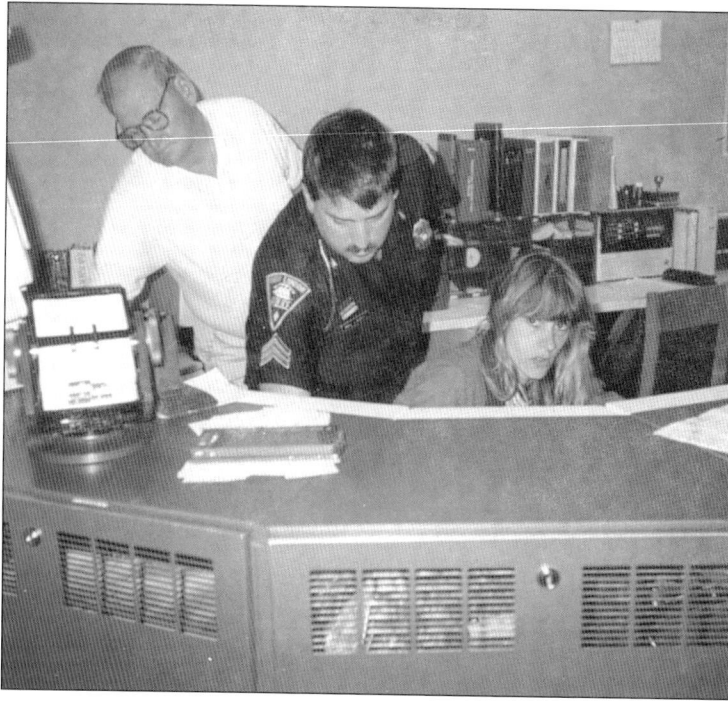

From left to right are bail commissioner Jack O'Connell, Sgt. William Lacey Jr., and dispatcher Joni Pockl. Lacking are modern headsets. Due to a lack of computers, most information was stored on paper. Teletype paperwork would be ripped off a dot-matrix printer and manually distributed. Phone numbers were kept in various flip-style holders, as shown to the left in the photograph. (Courtesy of retired Deputy Chief Marshall "Chip" Segar.)

Dispatcher Susan Snead is shown around the 1990s using a landline telephone. In front of her is a microphone used to radio officers on patrol. A similar microphone is used by dispatchers in 2018. Surrounding her are multiple computer screens for various aspects of tracking BOLOs or "Be On the LookOut." (Photograph by Sgt. William F. Brown.)

Inside the New London Police Headquarters–Communications Center is longtime dispatcher Timothy O'Neill, who manned the fire and police dispatch lines. (Photograph by Sgt. William F. Brown.)

From left to right are Wayne T. Vendetto (former mayor, city council member, and sheriff), Donald Sloan (retired chief), attorney Robert Martin (appointed judge and whose father was a high sheriff in New London County), and John Pearson (retired captain). Vendetto, Sloan, and Officer William D. Dittman Sr. were on the design-development committee for the existing police headquarters, dedicated in 1985. (Courtesy of the retired Capt. John W. Pearson family.)

In the Naval Underwater Sound Lab and Fort Trumbull neighborhood, in February 1984, local and state police officers and protestors line up facing each other when the USS *Georgia* was commissioned. From closest to the camera are New London officers William Lacey Jr., William D. Dittman Sr., Les Smith Jr., Patricia Leiteau, and Wayne Monty. (Courtesy of Sr. Sgt. Kevin McBride and the Paskewich family.)

Officer Douglass Williams fills out a report on paper. Note the leather jacket and longer sideburns that were still fashionable in 1986. His father, Doug, was a special officer who would augment the department on an as-needed basis, and he was the department's bicycle mechanic. Williams is an Air Force Vietnam veteran. (Courtesy of the New London Police Union.)

In 1990, the police department was authorized 100 full-time employees with a fleet of 30 vehicles and a helicopter shared with local municipalities. To work at the department in 1994, applicants needed two years of college and had to pass a barrage of tests. If hired, officers had to attend and pass a 14-week resident program at Connecticut Municipal Police Training Academy followed by an 18-month probationary period.

NEW LONDON
CONNECTICUT

Your future awaits ...

Officer Les Smith Jr. (left) is shown on patrol with Officer Ed Chmielewski. Chmielewski served as a sergeant and worked as a DARE (Drug Abuse Resistance Education) officer before going on to become a juvenile (JV) probation officer. (Courtesy of Les Smith Jr.)

From left to right are Officers Mark White, Roger Baker, and Marshall "Chip" Segar in 1990. Baker is currently a master patrol officer and union treasurer. Segar retired as the deputy chief and is an Army combat veteran of the First Gulf War in Iraq. (Courtesy of the New London Police Union.)

This squad in the 1990s was made up of, from left to right, (first row) Officers Greg Moreau, Jeffrey Kalolo, Patricia Leiteau, William Pero, Clayton Sizer, and Douglass Williams; (second row) Russell Cavanaugh, John F. Crowley, Sgt. Kenneth W. Edwards Jr., Sgt. William Lacey Jr. (acting lieutenant), Sgt. John Mattson, John Manavas, and Edmund Hedge. A copy of this photograph was placed on a plaque and given to retiring Lt. Gordon Dickens. (Courtesy of Lt. Jeffrey Kalolo.)

Officer Jeffrey Newlin (left) rides a Harley Davidson motorcycle and Officer Jeffrey Kalolo is on a Kawasaki motorcycle in 1996. (Courtesy of Lt. Jeffrey Kalolo.)

Julio Rogers maintained the vehicles for the New London Police Department for 20 years during the 1980s and 1990s, retiring in early 2000s. Just before he began, in 1978, new air-conditioned cruisers and an additional scooter were purchased, and the existing vehicles were repainted.

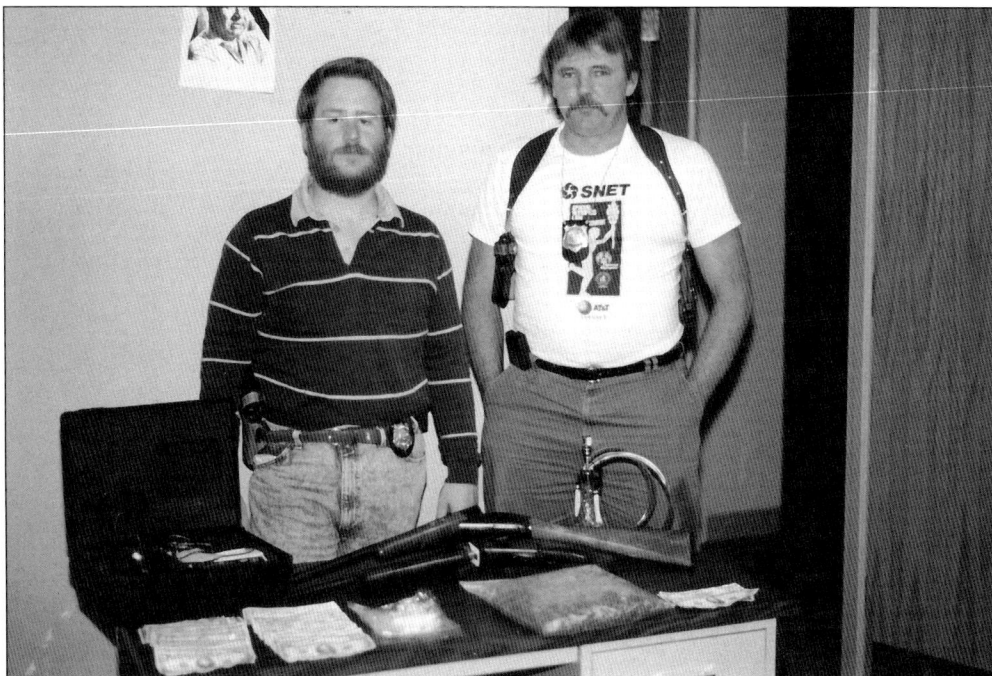

Vice and intelligence officers Michael Lacey (left) and Les Smith Jr. (right) are pictured with evidence from an arrest in October 1989. Smith, a Vietnam veteran, pioneered the department's vice and intelligence section, was undercover for several years, was a K-9 officer, and patrolled on foot and motorcycle. He retired after 33 years as a master patrol officer. (Courtesy of Kenneth W. Edwards Jr.)

In 1985, officers march in a parade on Main Street in Niantic, Connecticut. From left to right are (first column) Wayne Monty and handler William Nott Jr. with Thunder; (second column) Kenneth W. Edwards Jr. and handler Eric Deltgen with Bandit. Handler Deltgen patrolled with two other dogs during his tenure: Rocky and Shaka. Nott also patrolled with Phoenix. Nott retired from New London and Ledyard Police Departments. (Courtesy of the New London Police Union.)

Officer Phillip Fazzino is seen in 1993. He was the youth officer and provided focused work on DARE. He now works as a supervisory inspector with the state's attorney's office. (Courtesy of Phillip Fazzino.)

Officer Michael Gaska is pictured here. His generation of officers in the 1980s–1990s were able to use computers called mobile data terminals in their patrol cars and communicate with dispatchers. Just prior to this period, officers would haul the criminal to call boxes to call for a pickup or would use a pay phone to dial 911 to reach dispatch. (Courtesy of Kenneth W. Edwards Jr.)

Sgt. William F. Brown, a beloved member of the department, is shown handcuffed by his squad to the flagpole behind headquarters. He was the unofficial photographer for the department and sadly passed away just before this book began to take shape. His squad, from left to right, are Eric Deltgen, Jeffrey Kalolo, Edmund Hedge, Sergeant Brown, and Greg Moreau; behind Sergeant Brown are Russell Cavanaugh, Roger Baker, and Patricia Leiteau. In 1993, residents of New London formed a watch group, Let It Stop Now (LISN), that was the forerunner to the neighborhood watch groups in the city. In 1994, parents could bring their children to have photographs and fingerprints taken and were provided a book to store the information in through the efforts of the officers and Citizens Bank. In 1995, New London Telephone Employees Federal Credit Union donated bears that officers provided to children as a means of comfort. Still in effect today are child-safety seat programs with fitting stations, started with efforts by Officer Hedge. (Courtesy of the Sgt. William F. Brown family.)

Officer Robert Pickett is on a bicycle outside the front door of police headquarters at 5 Governor Winthrop Boulevard and Eugene O'Neill Drive. In May 1994, the bicycle patrol began through the efforts of the officers and local businesses. Olympic Sporting Goods, Iron Horse Bicycle, and Capitol Uniforms assisted with making retrofits to the bikes as well as getting the uniforms. (Courtesy of retired Lt. William Lacey Jr.)

Sgt. Joseph Weymouth and 12 others were hired as supernumeraries in 1976. Two years later, he was hired as a regular or full-time patrolman, and he was promoted to sergeant in March 1987. He passed away off duty in May 2006. Officers continue to talk about his foot chase for almost three miles from Ocean Beach Park to Willetts Avenue, where he finally caught the suspect. At the beginning of his career, there was the blizzard of 1976, which closed most of the state, the Sunday blue laws in Connecticut were repealed, and the country celebrated the bicentennial of the American Revolution. (Courtesy of the New London Police Department.)

A youth group, its escorts, and officers pose in front of the *Lettie G. Howard*, a schooner that sailed for OpSail 2000 out of South Seaport Museum in New York City with Capt. Kenneth W. Edwards Jr. (center). Officer Anthony Nolan is at top left with a police department ball cap on. Nolan dedicates extensive time to participating with city youth groups and is a member of the city council. (Courtesy of Kenneth W. Edwards Jr.)

A New London Police boat patrols the harbor during OpSail 2000. The Thames River boasts one of three deepwater ports in the state and allows for access to land and rail for many pleasure, commercial, and military vessels. (Courtesy of the New London Police Union.)

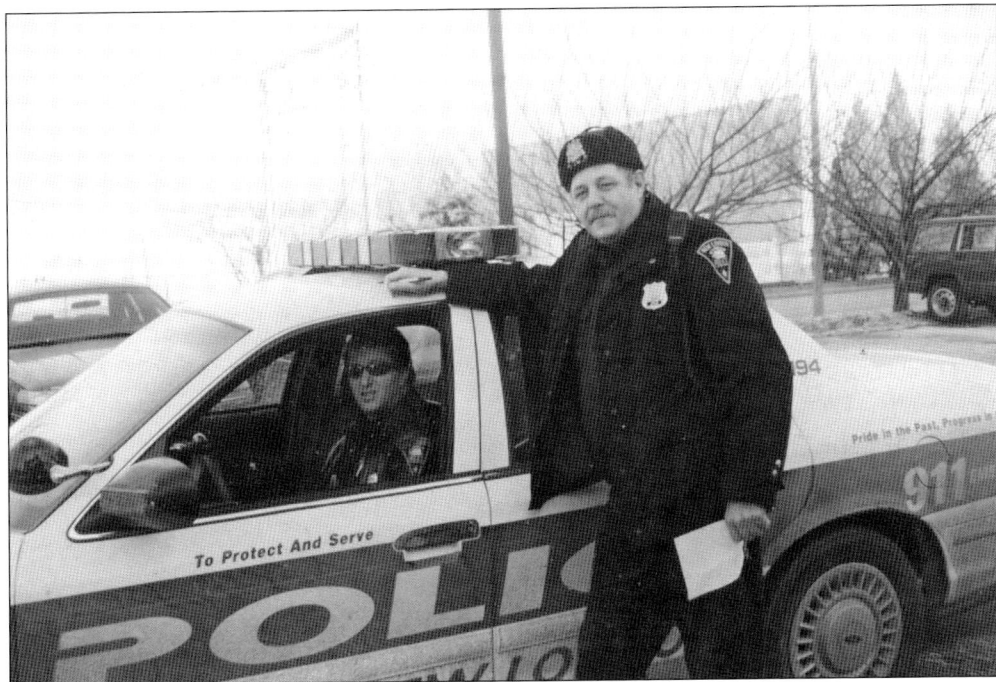

Officer Charles Percy sits inside and Officer Douglass Williams stands outside the police cruiser. In this January 2001 photograph, Williams is shown wearing a winter uniform cap. (Photograph by Sgt. William F. Brown.)

Officer Lawrence Lee is pictured with a New London Police patrol car around 2000. Lee began his career in 1995. It is unknown what he is pointing at, but for decades, until around the 1960s, officers would have their photographs taken while pointing to where a slip-and-fall or crime was committed. (Courtesy of the New London Police Union.)

NEW LONDON POLICE CRISIS INTERVENTION TEAM

New London Police C.I.T. Officers will wear this distinctive patch on the left sleeve of their uniforms.

C.I.T.

In 2001, crisis intervention team cards, like the ones shown here, were handed out to citizens. Based off an existing program in Tennessee, Capt. Kenneth W. Edwards Jr. and Lt. Marshall "Chip" Segar spearheaded the New London Police Department program, which was one of only 10 started in the country at this time. The flame-with-wing emblem was replicated for patrol officers, dispatchers, and detectives to wear as a patch, and later, a pin was authorized.

CALL 911 FOR EMERGENCIES

The Crisis Intervention Team is is designed to provide Emergency Police Assistance to consumers of Psychiatric Services. C.I.T. Officers are specially trained and can help you in a time of need. **Please Call**!

447-5269 ext. 0

Captain Ken Edwards ▪ Lieutenant Chip Segar
Sergeant Tim Hesney ▪ Sergeant Greg Moreau
Sergeant Brian Wright ▪ Detective Frank Jarvis
Officer Kevin Barney ▪ Officer Tyrone Baskett
Officer Todd Bergeson ▪ Officer Sean Dautrich
CPO William Edwards ▪ Officer Matthew Galante
Officer Darwin Garnett ▪ Officer Kevin McBride
Officer Humberto Morales ▪ Officer Anthony Nolan
Officer Deana Nott ▪ Dispatcher Lewis Cameron
Dispatcher Patricia Nunes ▪ Dispatcher Robin Schwarze

A grant through the United Way with training sponsored by Community Mental Health Services of Southeastern Connecticut helped to dispatch a member of the crisis intervention team (CIT) to any call with a mentally or emotionally upset citizen. A special patch was worn by officers to provide a visible presence of trained law enforcement officers who understand the challenges of getting proper services. (Courtesy of Kenneth W. Edwards Jr.)

Activist and state representative Ernest Hewitt (left) and Capt. Kenneth W. Edwards Jr. are shown in this c. 2013 photograph. In the 1990s, their work through a landmark case of citizen action forced a seedy hotel on Coleman Street to clean up its customer base because it devalued the neighborhood. Grants provided police training and patrols, leading to a decrease in crime of drugs and blight. (Courtesy of the New London Police Union.)

Officer Brian Wright sits to the left and Sgt. Timothy Hesney sits behind his desk in the shift commander's officer inside the Governor Winthrop Boulevard headquarters building in June 2001. (Photograph by Sgt. William F. Brown.)

Sgt. Dominic Bonano is shown walking through the back lot towards the headquarters at 5 Governor Winthrop Boulevard. Miscellaneous items he is carrying could be property out of a towed vehicle that would be kept in evidence for safekeeping. In the background is General Dynamics Electric Boat. (Courtesy of the New London Police Union.)

Sgt. Michael Strecker, shown in dress blues, is next to citizen and city council member John Maynard in 2008. Strecker served with the US Army. He retired from the police department as a senior sergeant in June 2015 after 26 years on patrol with vice, and he worked with the US Marshals Office. Notice the flip phone on Maynard's belt. (Courtesy of the New London Police Union.)

Lt. Stephen Colonis is smiling in this c. 2000 photograph. In 1976, the city council honored him for rescuing a woman being held against her will. Also honored in 1976 by the city council for their police work were patrolmen Gary Brown, Terry K. "T.K." Brown, and Robert Lee. Lee was honored for his work within the Eastern Regional Crime Squad. (Photograph by Sgt. William F. Brown.)

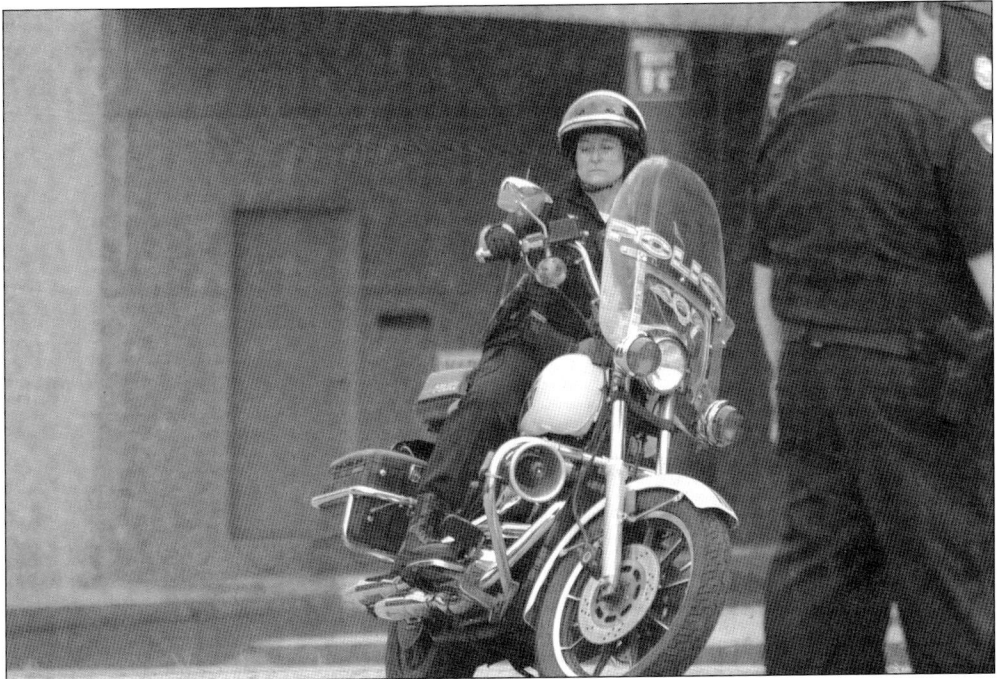

Officer Patricia Kehler rides a New London Police Department motorcycle in 2009. She successfully completed the difficult Connecticut State Police course for motorcycle police officers. Her blue line continues through her daughter, who serves as a Waterford police officer. (Courtesy of Les Smith Jr.)

Officer Matthew A. Galante IV is shown in 2008 with his dog Ike. Members of the public and businesses helped to support the K-9 program over the years. He and Ike received the Daniel Wasson Memorial K-9 Award in 2008. In 2003 and 2004, Officer Huberto Morales and K-9 Niko received the award. In 1998 and 1999, Officer Gregory Williams and K-9 Nero received the award. (Courtesy of Matthew A. Galante IV.)

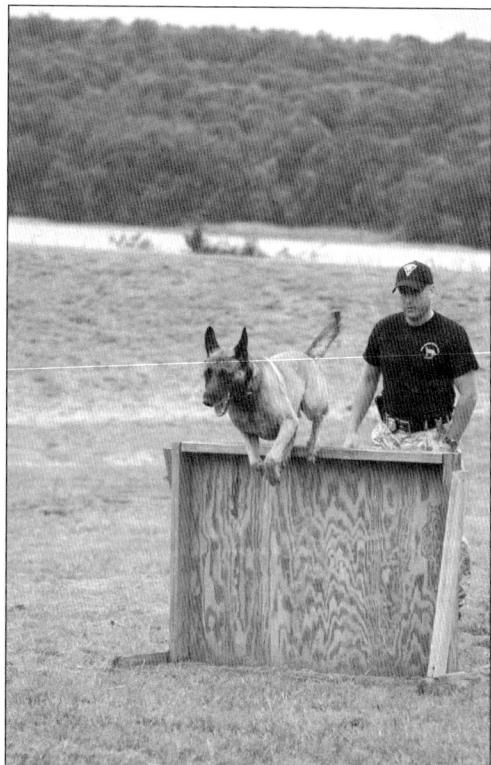

Investigator Todd Lynch and his Belgian Malinois K-9 Jasper are shown in 2009. In 1995, while serving as a Connecticut state trooper, Lynch and his K-9 Uriah received the Daniel Wasson Memorial K-9 Award. After retiring from the Connecticut State Police, Lynch joined New London. Since joining the department, one of his dogs has assisted him by jumping from his cruiser and coming to his aid during a traffic stop. (Photograph by Danielle Jewett; courtesy of the Officer John Michaud family.)

Officer John Michaud and his German shepherd K-9 Buck are shown at right in 2009. Handler Michaud was training Buck to jump over and through barriers as well as climb under posts. Dogs are used to track suspects, locate drugs, and perform vehicle searches. Handler and dog must be physically fit to run distances with many obstacles. (Photograph by Danielle Jewett; courtesy of the Officer John Michaud family.)

Pictured from left to right are officer/handler Christopher Bunkley and his K-9 Iris and K-9 Jesse and his officer/handler Joseph Kondash. Both dogs are Belgian Malinois. This photograph was taken in January 2018 on graduation day after approximately 11 weeks of training. Funding for the dogs is provided by city, except for the initial purchase from funds donated by citizens. (Photograph by Officer Daniel Lane; courtesy of Officer Joseph Kondash.)

Pictured from left to right in 2010 Capt. William D. Dittman Sr., Sgt. George Potts, and Sgt. Kevin Barney. All have retired and serve with the Mashantucket-Pequot Native American Tribal Police Department, with Dittman as chief of police. While with New London, Dittman worked on the building committee and assisted with the transfer from Union Street to Governor Winthrop Boulevard in 1985. (Courtesy of Les Smith Jr.)

Capt. Richard West is shown in the existing building at 5 Governor Winthrop Boulevard when it was first completed in 1985. He was instrumental in ensuring the upgrade to a modern communications system. (Courtesy of Kenneth W. Edwards Jr.)

This c. 2000 photograph shows Tueller Drill Training for law enforcement officers to keep their skills sharp for close-up knife attacks. Notice there are evaluators not wearing gear who will provide feedback about the training. (Courtesy of the New London Police Union.)

This car was seized from a drug dealer in the 1990s and repurposed as a bulletin board for others to learn "Don't Do Drugs." Officers were teaching children to say no to strangers. *Police Beat* was on public access television and was hosted by Officers Kenneth W. Edwards Jr. and Ed Chmielewski. (Courtesy of Kenneth W. Edwards Jr.)

Brass buttons are shown with the inscription "New London Police" and the city coat of arms of a ship with the Latin motto *Mare liberum*, meaning "Freedom of the Seas." They were first worn by officers in 1907, according to the *Day* newspaper, and were made by the Waterbury Button Company. Many wives contributed to the success of their husbands' appearances by polishing them and replacing them after the wool uniforms were returned from the dry cleaner. Many wives gave up jobs to stay home and run the household and raise children. Families formed their lives around the force and were part of formal balls as well as informal gatherings hosted within their homes. It was common to have one vehicle, and the officers would come out of work to families waiting in cars for them. Physicians talked to officers and their spouses about stressors of law enforcement causing illness and to anticipate a grieving process upon retirement. A debt of gratitude is owed to the spouses for their dedication. (Courtesy of Joan Corcoran McIntire and Kenneth W. Edwards Jr.)

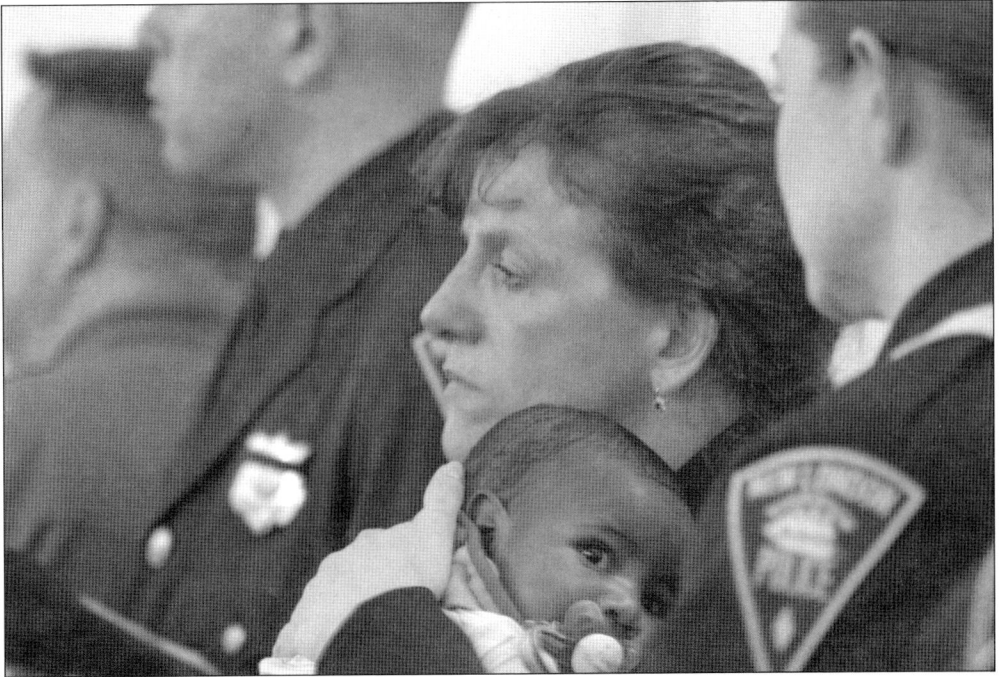

Officer Deana Nott is shown holding a baby during the 2007 funeral service for her colleague Raheem Carter. Carter's two-year career was cut short before succumbing to cancer at age 25. Nott and her husband, a city firefighter, have cared for children in their home for mothers who have been arrested. Her father and brother were officers in Waterford and East Lyme, respectively. (Courtesy of the New London Police Union.)

Joe Olivero (retired) is shown during a fundraiser police-versus-firefighters softball game for the Juliana Valentine McCourt Children's Education Fund. The goal is to help children with their self-esteem and cultural understanding. Juliana and her mother, Ruth, were killed while riding in an airplane that hit one of World Trade Center Towers on September 11, 2001. They were residents of New London. Olivero served in the US Marine Corps. (Courtesy of retired Lt. William Lacey Jr.)

Officer John F. Crowley served with the force from 1965 to 1994. He wears a whistle on his uniform and No. 99 on his cover. In early days on the force, it was not uncommon for officers to change badge numbers or wear a cap with a different number on it. Supernumeraries had to wear what was available. His son Steven followed in his footsteps. (Courtesy of the New London Police Department.)

Steven Crowley retired in January 2016 as a captain. In the photograph below from 2010, Capt. Steven Crowley (left) stands in front of Lt. Brian Wright. On the right, from front to rear, are Officer Richard Cable, Sgt. Lawrence M. Keating, and Det. Keith Crandall. They have lined up as part of the color guard prior to the start of a promotion ceremony. (Courtesy of the New London Police Union.)

Pictured from left to right in this c. 1973–1974 photograph are Clemente Delacruz, Axel Bergeson, and Grover A. Wigglesworth. In January 1973, Delacruz and Bergeson were sworn in as new patrol officers. Sadly, Lieutenant Bergeson passed away off duty in 1995. Wigglesworth served from 1971 to 1973 and left to join the Marines; he was medically discharged in 1977 after a helicopter crash. (Courtesy of the Bergeson family.)

Brothers Capt. Todd Bergeson (left) and Det. Joshua Bergeson are shown in 2017. Both officers followed in the path of their father, Axel. All three served in the US Marine Corps (Axel and Joshua as combat veterans) before joining the New London Police Department. (Courtesy of the Bergeson family.)

Retired MPO Michael Hedge is shown sitting at one of several typewriters under a shelf holding a dozen forms to choose from. A landline, with push buttons, hangs from the wall above a two-hole punch that used to keep papers in binders or clipboards. He served from 1985 to 2013 with his brother Edmund, shown at left. (Courtesy of Kenneth W. Edwards Jr.)

In 1980, retired traffic officer and MPO Edmund Hedge sits on a Harley Davidson the day it arrived, the first one at the department since the Roger DuPont era of the 1950s. Hedge, who included Navy personnel in motorcycle safety classes, retired in 2006 after 39 years of service. Other motorcycle officers in the 1980s were Clemente Delacruz, William D. Dittman Sr., Les Smith Jr., and Eric Deltgen. (Courtesy of the New London Police Union.)

Brothers patrolman Michael Lacey (left) and Sgt. William Lacey Jr. (right) are pictured outside headquarters at the 5 Governor Winthrop building around the 1980s. Dedicated service to the City of New London runs in the Lacey family. Michael retired as a captain and William as a lieutenant. Their father, William Lacey Sr., retired after 34 years as a lieutenant from the New London Fire Department. (Courtesy of the New London Police Union.)

Seated in this c. 2000 photograph is retired dispatcher Robin Schwarze. Standing to the right is her daughter second-generation dispatcher Tiffany Shultz. Standing to the left is dispatcher Kerry Lynch, whose brother Todd serves on the force. (Courtesy of the New London Police Union.)

A modern mobile command unit with the license plate "NO DUI" is shown on the left at Williams and Broad Streets in 2018. This unit can process DUIs and is the command center for large events. To the right is an SUV. There are automated traffic lights around Williams Park, but Sr. Sgt. Lawrence M. Keating manually directs traffic due to a car accident.

The police headquarters–communications center building was erected between 1981 and 1985 at 5 Governor Winthrop Boulevard and Eugene O'Neill Drive (formerly Main Street). This picture shows the walk-in entrance for the public.

National Police Week brought out volunteers in 2016 to help Officer Ryan Soccio beautify the front of the New London Police substation at 40 Truman Street. Other events that foster interaction with the public are Coffee with a Cop at various restaurants in town. Soccio serves the city as the crime prevention and traffic officer. (Courtesy of Officer Ryan Soccio.)

In 2013, Officer Joshua Bergeson assists wildlife. In addition to domestic dogs and cats, modern officers have helped round up a goat, an alligator, raccoons, opossums, skunks, and seagulls. The wildlife more worrisome to citizens have been foxes, bobcats, and coyotes roaming unabashedly. A campaign was launched in 2016 to educate people about keeping small pets and children closely supervised at all times. (Courtesy of the Bergeson family.)

Matthew Joslyn stands in front of one of the police vehicles he works on at the maintenance garage in 2018. He is a City of New London equipment mechanic in the mechanical maintenance department. In addition to the traditional vehicles, the department inventory included an electric buggy donated by Cross Sound Ferry and the Wronowski family.

This pickup truck is used for traffic services. The license plate reads "BUKL-UP." Officers in the late 2000s handed out business cards to educate citizens of their rights if they feel they have been racially profiled with online links: www.ct.gov/opm/cjppd/racialprofiling or www.ctrp3.org. (Courtesy of the New London Police Department.)

Officer Stephen Perry, shown in 2018, is one of the most recent officers in the department. He made a lateral transfer from New Haven into New London. In 2018, there would be morale boosters such as No-Shave November, allowing officers to participate in widely accepted social causes such as raising awareness for cancer. Officers were allowed to wear neatly trimmed beards for the month.

Officer Juan Cruz Jr., pictured in 2018, is one of the most recent officers in the department. He made a lateral transfer from Hartford into his native New London. An event he may be found participating in locally and with the support of the Capano family in their Shop Rite parking lot is Pack the Paddy Wagon; food is collected and donated to the local Gemma E. Moran Food Center for Thanksgiving meals.

Officer Richard Cable (who served in the Connecticut Army National Guard) is pictured around 2000 on State Street with the Thames River behind him. Gone are the days of horse-and-buggies and dirt roads lit with oil lamps that can be seen in the photograph on page 11. The old-fashioned streetlights are electric, and the light bulbs have gone from filaments to light-emitting diodes (LEDs). Gone also are the days of the long wool coats, nightsticks, and belts that carried the old revolvers. Modern officers may holster a magazine-loaded handgun, a can of pepper spray, a taser or electronic defense weapon (EDW), a baton, and handcuffs. He communicates through a handheld microphone at the top of his zippered jacket so he can radio back-and-forth to headquarters and other officers and has at least one cellphone with access to the Internet. The patch he wears on his shoulder and the shield on his chest and hat, along with a need for a comfortable pair of shoes, have remained the same for New London police officers for 150 years. (Courtesy of the New London Police Union.)

Five

NEW LONDON POLICE DEPARTMENT 150TH-YEAR GROUP PHOTOGRAPHS

Authorized commemorative badges celebrating 150 years of continuous police presence are worn by officers in 2018.

Chief of New London Police Peter G. Reichard took charge of the department in 2017.

From left to right are Capt. Todd Bergeson (uniform services), Capt. Brian Wright (investigative services), and Capt. Lawrence J. Keating Jr. (support services).

The administrative assistants, from left to right, are (first row) police secretary Lori Robinson, assistant to the police chief Jennifer Martley, and police secretary Dixie Woods; (second row) records clerk Bethany Huntley and Laila Andersen. Missing is Yvonne Taylor.

The dispatchers are, from left to right, Timothy DeVeau, Richard Waselik, Kerry Lynch, and Jamie DeGunia. Missing are Jennifer Candelario, Katelin Greatsinger, Michael Mariano, Tiffany Shultz, and Joseph Nott.

From left to right are Sr. Sgt. Gregory Moreau (support services supervisor), Sr. Sgt. Lawrence M. Keating (training), Officer John Green (evidence), and Officer Ryan Soccio (traffic services and crime prevention).

The investigative services division is made up of, from left to right, (first row) Investigators Todd Lynch, Joseph Pelchat, Ryan Griffin, and Justin Lawrie; (second row) Det. Sgt. Cornelius Rodgers and Dets. William Pero, Keith Crandall, Christopher Kramer, Richard Curcuro, and Joshua Bergeson. Missing is Investigator Jeremy Zelinski.

The day-shift officers are, from left to right (first row) Deana San Juan Nott; Joseph Buzzelli; K-9 handler Christopher Bunkley; and MPOs Daniel Jaramillo and Joshua Malaro; (second row) Lt. Jeffrey Kalolo; Sr. Sgt. Scott Johnson; Officers Brendan Benway, Eric Hulland, Melissa Schafranski, and Kurt Lavimoniere; MPO Roger Baker; Officer Christopher White; and MPO Lawrence Lee. Missing are Sr. Sgt. Russell Cavanaugh and MPO James Suarez.

The afternoon-shift officers are, from left to right, (first row) Zachariah Kelley; Lucas DelGrosso, Alexander Dyer; Jorden Salas; Jeffrey Nichols; and Darrin O'Mara; (second row) Lt. Matthew A. Galante IV; Sgt. Charles Flynn; Officer Jeremiah Lamont; Sgt. Max Bertsch; Officers Ashley James, Michael Lewis, Matthew Cassiere, Christopher Valerio, and Marco Zandri; and K-9 handler Joseph Kondash. Missing is Sgt. Kristy Christina.

The midnight-shift officers are, from left to right, (first row) MPO Scott Jones; Officer Anthony Nolan; Doreen Coe; Thomas Northup; K-9 handler John Michaud; and Officer Richard Stringer; (second row) Lt. Robert Pickett; Sgt. Tyrone "Kyle" Baskett; Sgt. Brian Laurie; Officers Mikhail Liachenko, Dustin Adkins, and Richard Cable; MPO Wayne Neff; and Officer Ryan Linderson. Missing are Sr. Sgt. Kevin McBride and Officer Patricia Kehler.

Sr. Sgt. Kevin McBride (middle) has been with the force for more than 24 years and was serving his 20th year as a senior chief investigator (IVSC/E-8) and special agent in the US Coast Guard Reserve Investigative Service when squad photographs were taken. (Courtesy of the New London Police Union.)

Investigator Jeremy Zelinski was on a special assignment when squad photographs were taken. He was the Veterans of Foreign Wars Officer of the Year in 2013. (Courtesy of Jeremy Zelinski.)

Assistant animal control officers (ACOs) seen here are Kelly Duso (left) and Tonya Kloiber. Recently retired Michael Martin is not shown. From their office and kennels at Bates Woods, they investigate reports of stray, rabid, and injured animals. According to retired city clerk Clark van der Lyke, New London was first in the country to issue dog licenses in the 1700s.

The New London Police Department on May 22, 2018, outside the New London Police building at 5 Governor Winthrop Boulevard, is, from left to right, (first row) Chief Peter G. Reichard; Lt. Jeffrey Kalolo; Sgt. Brian Laurie; MPO Wayne Neff; Officers John Green, John Michaud, Ryan Soccio, Ashley James, and Thomas Northup; Investigator Todd Lynch; Officer Deana Nott; MPO Lawrence Lee; and Officers Matthew Cassiere, Richard Cable, and Doreen Coe; (second row) Capt. Lawrence J. Keating Jr.; Lt. Robert Pickett; Sgt. Charles Flynn; Officers Jeremiah Lamont and Ryan Linderson; Investigators Ryan Griffin, Justin Lawrie, and Joseph Pelchat; Officers Jorden Salas, Jeffrey Nichols, and Richard Stringer; Det. Joshua Bergeson; and Officers Brendan Benway and Melissa Schafranski; (third row) Capt. Todd Bergeson; Lt. Matthew A. Galante IV; Sgt. Max Bertsch; Officer Mikhail Liachenko; K-9 handler Christopher Bunkley; Officer Michael

Lewis; MPO Daniel Jaramillo; and Officers Christopher White, Dustin Adkins, Lucas DelGrosso, Joseph Buzzelli, Zachariah Kelley, Christopher Valerio, and Darrin O'Mara; (fourth row) Capt. Brian Wright; Sr. Sgt. Scott Johnson; Sgt. Cornelius Rodgers; Officer Anthony Nolan; K-9 handler Joseph Kondash; Officers Kurt Lavimoniere, Joshua Malaro, and Eric Hulland; MPO Roger Baker; Officers Alexander Dyer and Marco Zandri; and MPO Scott Jones; (fifth row) Sgt. Tyrone "Kyle" Baskett; Sr. Sgt. Lawrence M. Keating; and Dets. William Pero, Keith Crandall, Christopher Kramer, and Richard Curcuro. Missing are MPO James Suarez, Sr. Sgt. Russell Cavanaugh, Sr. Sgt. Kevin McBride, Sgt. Kristy Christina, Officers Patricia Kehler and Joshua Malaro, and Investigator Jeremy Zelinski.

DISCOVER THOUSANDS OF LOCAL HISTORY BOOKS FEATURING MILLIONS OF VINTAGE IMAGES

Arcadia Publishing, the leading local history publisher in the United States, is committed to making history accessible and meaningful through publishing books that celebrate and preserve the heritage of America's people and places.

Find more books like this at
www.arcadiapublishing.com

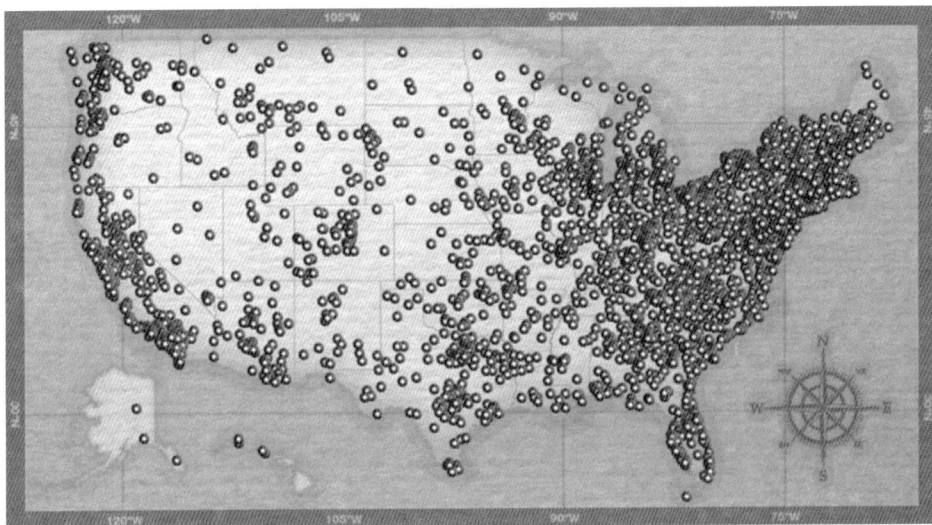

Search for your hometown history, your old stomping grounds, and even your favorite sports team.

Consistent with our mission to preserve history on a local level, this book was printed in South Carolina on American-made paper and manufactured entirely in the United States. Products carrying the accredited Forest Stewardship Council (FSC) label are printed on 100 percent FSC-certified paper.

MADE IN THE USA